401
Ways
to Get
Your Kids
to Work
at Home

401
Ways
to Get
Your Kids
to Work
at Home

Bonnie Runyan McCullough
Susan Walker Monson

**Illustrations by Laura Hammond
with Bonnie McCullough and Susan Monson**

St. Martin's Griffin
New York

Dedicated to the nine children
who will be judged by the things
their mothers wrote:
Bobette, Laura, Wesley,
Becky, and Madison McCullough;
Melea, Eric, Sarah, and Marc Monson.

ACKNOWLEDGMENT

Special thanks to Barbara Anderson, our editor
at St. Martin's Press; to our readers,
David H. Monson and Glenna Hansen Berg;
to our husbands, Robert McCullough and
David H. Monson; and to our children for their
support and encouragement.

Library of Congress Cataloging in Publication Data

McCullough, Bonnie Runyan.
    401 ways to get your kids to work at home.
    1. Family life education. 2. Home economics.
I. Monson, Susan Walker. II. Title. III. Title: Four
hundred and one ways to get your kids to work at home.
IV. Title: Four hundred one ways to get your kids to work at home.
HQ10.M4 1982   646.7'8   81-14548
ISBN 0-312-29993-1   AACR2

Design by Mina Greenstein
20 19 18 17 16

Contents

Introduction

Today money is tight, time is rushed, and most of us feel we could use some help at home. But how many parents have tapped the closest potential resource, their children? "It's a marvelous theory," we hear, "however it takes more time than it saves." Parents might be able to do a task better and faster than their children, but should they? No. We think it is a good idea for our children to work at home because children need to learn to work and parents need their help.

By the time your children reach eighteen years of age, they will have spent 32,234 hours under your guidance and training. Consider that it takes only 2,100 hours of classroom and outside study time to complete a bachelor's degree in college and half that time to learn some skilled trades. Your home has sixteen times more teaching hours than does the university. What do you want to do with this time?

Think about your children walking out the door, on their own! We assume they can cope with the everyday challenges of living, but should we? We assume they know about basic household duties and maintenance, but do they? We assume they can efficiently prepare well-balanced, nutritious meals, but can they? We assume they have mastered some basic skills of orderliness with their personal belongings, but have they? We assume they will handle their earnings wisely, avoiding unnecessary debt, but will they? Too often parents let the chips fall where they may, hoping all will turn out for the best. Can we leave the basic teachings to chance? Is there a better way?

This book was written to share principles, strategies, and tips on how to help your children succeed in home assignments. B. F. Skinner discovered, through his experiments with pigeons, that he could get a bird to peck ten thousand times in hopes of getting a food-pellet reward. Children can manipulate adults to get the attention or the reward they seek. Like the pigeon, they try over and over again to get the reward whether it be positive or negative. We will show you how to turn the negative responses into positive responses that motivate the child to do what you think he or she should do, which, in this case is work at home.

In this book you're going to learn what skills a child should know at what age. You will learn how to teach those skills, and you will learn how to motivate your child to perform them. It seems that someone else can usually get a child to work better than the parent can, but the parent can role-play or dramatize the situation to make it fun and create the outside incentive to get the child to work. Stories, charts, games and techniques are offered to keep the child working until he or she has the maturity and inner desire to do so.

If you are looking for a trick to bring about immediate results right now, try the guessing game. Have the child put away ten items in a room and you guess what has been put away. To change the "drop-it" habit of children who leave coats, books, and personal belongings all over the central living areas of the house, initiate the "Eight o'clock Pick-up" as described on page 127. If your child's bedroom is the problem, turn directly to chapter nine to evaluate the cause or try using the bedroom inspection chart (page 150). Chapter twelve, titled 401 Ways to Get Your Child to Work at Home, offers many suggestions of tricks and principles to spark your creativity in getting your children to work in positive ways.

Other parts of this book, like Setting Goals, Knowing the Learning Seasons, or Getting Together, offer the theory behind establishing a strong family foundation to help rear responsibly independent children. This book will help focus attention on a workable plan for parents and children to follow in using those 32,234 teaching hours productively. It is intended as a guide to success in areas one might otherwise leave to happenstance. You may have to change some of your own actions and perhaps alter the physical set-up of the home environment to help the child improve.

It is not too late to start, no matter what the age of your child, although the methods and incentives may vary. Give yourself credit for what you have done. Your interest in this book shows you are already seeking to initiate some of these ideas. Leave behind any regrets for past mistakes. You have done the best you could with the tools you had at the time. We cannot promise that your children will take over the housework or even initiate any tasks on their own, but at least we can help you train them, so that when they do have their own homes, and the inner desire to keep them nice, they will have the skills to do so.

In a survey of 250 children, over ninety-seven percent honestly felt they should work at home. Let's teach them and give them the opportunity. Training children to work offers many rewards. For the children it adds greatly to their self-esteem and sense of belonging. They gain skills necessary for adult life, establish patterns of success that foster independence and self-reliance, and learn to work quickly and efficiently. There is a greater awareness of the value of things and more appreciation of efforts made by others. The parent is rewarded because part of the workload is lifted, the anger of feeling used is removed, and there is more time for the fun things of life. The parent feels a sense of success in preparing the child for the adult world, as the familiar phrase admonishes:

Catch me a fish and I'll eat today.
Teach me to fish and I'll eat the rest of my life.

1: Setting the Goals

When your children leave home to go out into the world on their own, what home skills will they be able to perform? If you could give each child fifty thousand dollars as he or she departs, would that be as valuable as if they had mastered some basic skills in preparation for adult life: The little things that have to be done every day even if they live to be 103? If young adults know how to clean a house and keep it that way, how to select and cook good food, or how to budget money, then they are released from the extra time it takes to learn these things when time is needed to concentrate on studies, career, or other areas of living.

Consider the case of a twenty-one-year-old girl named Annie who moved to Colorado hoping the dry climate would help clear up a health problem. When she drove up to her new apartment in her little compact car, she had her clothes and six thousand dollars' worth of debts. Her own parents had advised her to buy not a used but a brand-new car, a new sewing machine (she is learning to sew), a new piano (someday she hopes to play), and correspondence art lessons; all of these when her job paid minimum wage. Annie's lack of understanding of nutrition and how to cook soon affected her health. She struggled to read a city map. She had had so little experience in the world that it was easy for someone to take advantage of her. A friend called her from overseas, collect, and talked for twenty minutes. You guessed it! She did not know that collect meant she would pay for the call. All of these problems and a lack of preparation made her very discouraged. Is it possible that many of us are raising Annies?

As parents, if we do not have goals for our children an Annie is possible, and we cannot help them set goals if we have only a vague idea of what we wish them to achieve. You may ask, "Do we as parents have the right to decide on the goals our children should achieve?" Our answer is yes, because once the parent establishes the parameters in which the child can safely act and develop skills for successfully meeting life's challenges, then the child's right to choose comes into play. The child usually does not have the maturity to set goals without these limits. Unfortunately, we usually give more careful planning to a two-week vacation than we do to the training of our children in the basic home living skills. As a parent, there are ways to prepare your child for the Big World whether they are two or twenty-two. During the eighteen years or so a child is in your home, you will be doing lots of things and going many places, so why not get full value from these experiences through goal setting, and plan your activities to provide the maximum instructional benefit for your children? The child's accomplishment of skills will improve self-image and give the confidence on which to build even more skills. Independent children can bounce back from crises and move forward while dependent children are more vulnerable to problems that can ruin their lives. You, the parent, will enjoy many rewards too; your sense of success develops, the workload is shared, and the child will be working with you rather than against you. Setting these goals will create more time for the parent and child to enjoy other things in life.

It is interesting to note that in a survey we took, asking 250 children about working at home, ninety-seven per cent felt they should help. Listen to the reasons they gave.

Children said they should help at home because:

"Then parents won't go nuts trying to do all the work by themselves."

"They make a lot or half of the mess in the house. They also are going to have a house someday, and they need to know how to clean and cook."

"It will be easier to get a job and support yourself."

"It gives you experience, gets you organized, prepares you for later life."

"Children have to learn responsibilities, because if they don't, when they grow up they will be lazy bums."

"Then we get all the work done so we can do the fun things."

"My mom and dad are divorced and my mom has always had a full-time job. Therefore, she needs our help. My sister and I (seventeen and twelve) don't expect her to do both."

"I think it forms good habits when the child becomes an adult."

"It helps Mom and Dad out because they are putting food on your plate."

As parents, we can become aware of methods that help the child see both what needs to be done and ways that create independence. For example, one youthful volleyball captain was so anxious for her team to win, that she began issuing constant commands. When a girl made a mistake, she told that girl exactly what should have been done. "You should hit it with your fist. Move up, you're back too far!" Within ten minutes this novice captain had every girl looking toward her, waiting for instructions before making a move. Some parents do this at home, telling the child each move to make. But we want the child to develop independence as well as obedience. There are seven steps in training independent children and getting them to work at home:

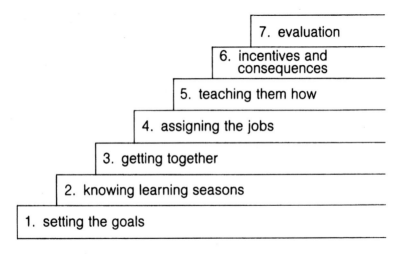

7. evaluation
6. incentives and consequences
5. teaching them how
4. assigning the jobs
3. getting together
2. knowing learning seasons
1. setting the goals

The first four are the groundwork done before telling the child to "get to work." The real fun is in teaching the child how to do a task and making up incentives that motivate. The rewards come regularly as the child learns skills and develops self-confidence. Before actually starting to teach, you need to decide where you and your child are going.

If you don't decide on your goals, you'll become like Alice in Wonderland, who was asked by the Cheshire Cat where she wanted "to get to." When Alice answered that she didn't "much care where," he said, "Then it doesn't much matter which way you go."

WHERE ARE YOU GOING?

It does matter which way we are going with our children. To help in goal setting, think how a school system might do it. Many schools have punch-out progress cards that move with the child from grade to grade, showing which skills in math and language arts the child has studied and passed. The list could look very discouraging to a first-grader, but as the child works day after day, concept upon concept, a great many things are learned. Wouldn't it be interesting to see what level your child would be on in "Home Living Skills"?

The following Home Progress Chart has been designed to help define what you hope your own children will have learned before leaving home. The chart is a beginning point and a recording sheet; reduce or expand it to meet your circumstances. Remember that, without being conscious of it, we often forget to teach the youngest child what we taught the older children out of necessity. Also, we neglect to teach boys some household jobs and girls some repair skills, assuming they will have a spouse to handle those omitted areas. But we suggest boys and girls will benefit from learning about both areas. Handicapped children should also learn as many skills as they can possibly master.

Although the chart basically includes household responsibilities, full support should be given to the child's school studies. You might also want to include some marketable skills and provide outside help from other teachers for typing, upholstering, electrical repairs, and the like.

Now go through the chart, deciding which skills you want your children to develop. There are many entries provided, but it may be more beneficial to choose three categories, look those over carefully, and decide on one skill that you would like to teach your child from each category; or you could choose three skills from only one category. If you have several children who are close in age you might work with them as a group, or you can teach one child now and the other children

HOME PROGRESS CHART

1. Write the child's initials next to the skill you want to teach. There is room for the initials of several children.

2. When the child has mastered the job, place a slash through the initials. [S̸M̸ Clean own drawers(6–14)]

3. The numbers printed after each skill represent the earliest age to introduce the skill and the age at which you can expect mastery. Of course, every child is different and you must be flexible with the ages, judging from your own experience, the facilities available, examples of friends and siblings, and the child's confidence and maturity.

4. Use the same chart for both girls and boys because we cannot insure the skills will be needed by only one gender.

Example:

Phyllis and her daughter (age ten) looked at the Home Progress Chart together and chose one skill from each of three different categories.

Category	Skill
Money Skills	Make a checking account deposit
Cooking	Select and prepare fresh fruits and vegetables
Navigation and Auto	Ride the city bus

By choosing only three skills to develop, they were not overwhelmed, and could begin meeting the goals immediately. Later in this chapter, we will explain the Three Teaching Elements (page 15) to help you be very specific about reaching your goals.

later. Some skills you will only introduce at this point and expect mastery later. Your children are introduced to a skill
when they have direct participation in the job through observing others doing it, asking questions about it, or helping with
part of it. They have mastery when they can independently
complete the task at least three times with success. Remember
that the Home Progress Chart is only a guide (not a test) to
help you set goals for your family. Some items listed may be
unimportant to you and there may be other skills you wish to
add. Be flexible and have fun evaluating and dreaming.

Personal Care Skills

_____ Put pajamas
away (2–4)

_____ Pick up toys (2–6)

_____ Undress self (2–4)

_____ Comb hair (2–5)

_____ Wash face, hands
(2–5)

_____ Brush teeth (2–5)

_____ Tidy up bedroom
(2–8)

_____ Dress self (3–6)

_____ Make own bed (3–7)

_____ Clean, trim nails (5–
10)

_____ Leave bathroom neat
after use (6–10)

_____ Wash and dry own
hair (7–10)

_____ Arrange for own
haircuts (10–16)

_____ Purchase own
grooming supplies
(11–18)

Clothing Care Skills

_____ Empty hamper, put
dirty clothes in
wash area (4–8)

_____ Put away clean
clothes (5–9)

_____ Clean own drawers
(6–14)

_____ Clean own closet (6–
16)

_____ Fold, separate clean
laundry (8–16)

_____ Hang clothes for
sun drying (8–16)

Clothing Care Skills

_____ Fold clothes neatly, without wrinkles (8–16)

_____ Polish shoes (8–18)

_____ Wash clothes in machine (9–16)

_____ Operate electric clothes dryer (9–16)

_____ Clean lint trap and washer filter (10–16)

_____ Shop for clothing (11–18)

_____ Basic spot removal —blood, oil, coffee, tea, soda, etc. (12–18)

_____ Waterproof shoes/ boots (12–18)

_____ Iron clothing (12–18)

_____ Hand-wash lingerie or woolens (12–18)

_____ Simple mending— buttons and holes (12–17)

_____ Sort clothes by color, dirt, fabric content (8–18)

_____ Take clothes for dry cleaning

_____ Simple sewing (12–18)

Household Skills

_____ Clear off own place at table (2–5)

_____ Wipe up a spill (3–10)

_____ Dust furniture (3–12)

_____ Set table (3–7)

_____ Clear table (3–13)

_____ Pick up trash in yard (4–10)

_____ Shake area rugs (4–8)

_____ Spot-clean walls (4–12)

_____ Wipe off door frames (4–12)

_____ Clean TV screen and mirrors (4–8)

_____ Feed pets (5–10)

_____ Clean toilet (5–8)

_____ Scour sink and tub (5–12)

_____ Empty wastebaskets (4–10)

_____ Sweep porches, patios, walks (4–10)

_____ Wipe off chairs (6–11)

Household Skills

_____ Know differences
and uses of var-
ious household
cleaners (6–14)

_____ Load and turn on
dishwasher (6–12)

_____ Empty diswasher
and put dishes
away (6–12)

_____ Wash and dry dishes
by hand (6–12)

_____ Clean combs,
brushes (6–8)

_____ Clean bathroom
(total) (6–12)

_____ Scrub or mop
floor (6–13)

_____ Use vacuum cleaner
(7–12)

_____ Clean pet cages and
bowls (7–13)

_____ Take written tele-
phone messages
(7–12)

_____ Use broom, dust-
pan (8–12)

_____ Vacuum upholstery
and drapes (8–14)

_____ Water house
plants (8–14)

_____ Water grass (8–14)

_____ Fold blankets neatly
(8–14)

_____ Wash car (8–16)

_____ Weed garden (9–13)

_____ Change bed linens
(10–13)

_____ Replace light bulbs,
understand watt-
age (10–15)

_____ Clean fireplace (10–
15)

_____ Polish silver-
ware (11–15)

_____ Replace fuse or know
where breakers
are (11–18)

_____ Oil squeaky
door (12–18)

_____ Change vacuum belt
and bag (12–15)

_____ Trim trees,
shrubs (12–18)

_____ Mow lawn (12–16)

_____ Polish wood furni-
ture (14–18)

_____ Wash windows (13–
18)

_____ Place long distance
calls (13–17)

_____ Place collect calls
(13–18)

_____ Unstop a drain with
chemicals or
plunger (13–18)

_____ Install a lock (14–
18)

_____ Change plug on
electric cord (14–
18)

Household Skills

_____ Scrub down walls (14–18)
_____ Wax a floor (14–18)
_____ Clean bathroom tile (14–18)
_____ Replace faucet washer (15–18)
_____ Use weather and all-purpose caulking (16–18)
_____ Know what to look for in home appliances (16–18)

Cooking Skills

_____ Know basic food groups and nutrition (5–14)
_____ Put groceries away (6–16)
_____ Make punch (6–9)
_____ Make a sandwich (6–12)
_____ Cook canned soup (7–12)
_____ Read a recipe (7–12)
_____ Measure properly (7–14)
_____ Make gelatin (7–12)
_____ Pack a cold lunch (7–12)
_____ Boil eggs (7–13)
_____ Scramble eggs (9–13)
_____ Distinguish between good and spoiled foods (10–18)
_____ Bake a cake from a mix (10–14)
_____ Cook frozen, canned vegetables (10–13)
_____ Mix pancakes (10–17)
_____ Read ingredient labels wisely (10–15)
_____ Plan balanced meal (10–15)
_____ Select and prepare fresh fruits and vegetables (10–18)
_____ Bake cookies (10–16)
_____ Bake muffins, biscuits (11–17)
_____ Make tossed salad (11–15)
_____ Make hot beverages (12–16)
_____ Fry hamburger (12–16)
_____ Broil a steak (12–16)
_____ Bake bread (12–17)
_____ Make fruit salad (13–15)
_____ Clean frost-free refrigerator (12–18)
_____ Make casserole (14–18)

Cooking Skills

_____ Clean oven and stove (15–18)

_____ Carve meat (15–18)

_____ Plan and shop for groceries for a week (15–18)

_____ Defrost refrigerator or freezer (15–18)

_____ Cook a roast (15–18)

_____ Fry a chicken (16–18)

Money Skills

_____ Know monetary denominations; penny, dime, etc. (5–12)

_____ Freedom to use small allowance (5–12)

_____ Make change and count your change (8–11)

_____ Compare quality and prices (8–12)

_____ Make savings or checking account deposit (10–18)

_____ Use a simple budget (12–18)

_____ Return item to store properly (14–18)

_____ Write a check (14–18)

_____ Balance checkbook (14–18)

_____ Understand what household bills must be paid; rent, electricity, water, telephone, etc. (15–18)

_____ Know how to properly use credit card (16–18)

Navigation and Auto Skills

_____ Know address (4–6)

_____ Know phone number (4–6)

_____ Clean interior of car (8–14)

_____ Ride bus or taxi (8–16)

_____ Oil a bicycle (9–14)

_____ Repair bicycle tire (10–15)

Navigation and Auto Skills

_____ Wash car properly (10–17)

_____ Read a map (7–14)

_____ Polish car (12–17)

_____ Fill car with gas (15–18)

_____ Check oil (15–18)

_____ Fill radiator (16–18)

_____ Change flat tire (16–18)

_____ Fill tires with air (16–18)

_____ Drive car (16–18)

Other Skills

_____ Make emergency call such as ambulance, police, fire department (5–12)

_____ Learn to swim (5–14)

_____ Check book out of library (6–10)

_____ Know emergency first-aid procedures (10–18)

_____ Understand uses of medicine and seriousness of overuse (10–18)

_____ Plan a small party (12–18)

_____ Properly hang something on wall (12–18)

_____ Know differences between latex, enamel paint, wood stains, and polyurethane (12–18)

_____ Paint a room (12–18)

_____ Type (14–18)

_____ Change furnace or air conditioner filter (14–18)

_____ Contact landlord with problem and follow through (14–18)

_____ Organize spring house cleaning (15–18)

_____ Clean water heater and if gas, light it (16–18)

_____ Repair wall holes with putty (16–18)

_____ Shampoo carpets (16–18)

_____ Arrange for services such as trash removal or extermination

Additional Skills

————— —————
————— —————
————— —————
————— —————

MAKE PLANS TO REACH YOUR GOALS

Filling out the Home Progress Chart will clarify the skills your child has mastered, the skills that need strengthening, and other skills you want your child to have. Now that you know where to begin, it is time to set goals. Consider the child's level of maturity: Can my child handle this skill physically, mentally, and emotionally? Consider the time demands: Is my child too busy for this with a heavy school schedule, dance or music recitals? Think about parental stress: Am I too tied up with overtime at work and the church social to organize? Remain flexible with the plans as circumstances change.

The school curriculum year, winter and spring breaks, and the longer summer vacation suggest possible scheduling boundaries and opportunities. During school, when children concentrate on studies, emphasize strengthening regular daily routines and simple one-day projects, like making a tossed salad or checking the oil in the car. Vacation times could be used to teach more complex skills like gardening, map reading, or sewing. In June, goals can be set and plans made for the skills you intend to integrate with summer fun. It helps to write down the plans for each child in the various categories like personal, household, money, and so forth. Use the back pages of this book or a special notebook for family goals.

Being aware of goals will help you take advantage of community organizations such as Scouts, 4-H, and their feeder groups. Jane can take sewing in 4-H. John can complete the

Personal Management Merit Badge in Scouts, with its emphasis on money management. The programs of these groups are achievement orientated, so children benefit doubly, learning the skills taught and receiving goal-setting training.

DEVELOP A REACHABLE GOAL

A beginning student teacher often complains about the tedious task of writing objectives for her new students. She soon learns, however, that the objective-writing process clarifies all dimensions of the goal. Later, this once burdensome chore becomes automatic. The new teacher learns that a goal is more attainable if it includes these three teaching elements: (1) desired behavior, (2) needed conditions, and (3) the expected standard. These three ingredients can apply in the home. You

THREE TEACHING ELEMENTS

Behavior or Action	What will be done? *Mark will dust the living room.*
Conditions	What equipment is needed? *He will use a dust cloth and spray polish from the "Maid Basket."* When will it be done? *Dusting will be done after breakfast on Saturday.*
Standard	How well should it be done? Who will check the work? *Mother will occasionally inspect and find no trace of dust on furniture.*

don't have to write out objectives and lesson plans like a teacher, but if you have trouble meeting your goal, it may be helpful to go back over these factors to see if you have missed one.

The actions, conditions, and standards vary with the age of the child and the difficulty of the task. For instance, dusting an open-space room with modern-style furniture does not require the same maturity or skill as dusting a room filled with antiques and knickknacks. Regardless of the job, if the child knows what is expected, has the necessary equipment, understands the specific time when it is to be done, and knows what the end result must be, the success is almost guaranteed. If you say completely what you mean, the child will usually do it.

Using this chart will help you include the three teaching elements in the goals that you set.

THREE TEACHING ELEMENTS

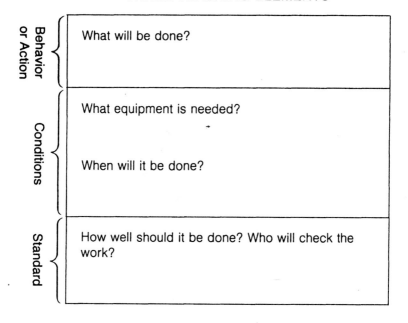

Behavior or Action	What will be done?
Conditions	What equipment is needed? When will it be done?
Standard	How well should it be done? Who will check the work?

GOAL-SETTING EXAMPLES

The following examples will clarify the effective use of the three teaching elements. Vicky decides that for her eight-year-old daughter, Shirley, setting the table, dusting the furniture, and weeding the flower beds are appropriate skills for the next three-month period. Since Vicky works full time, Saturdays will be her best training days. While driving home from a piano lesson Vicky says, "Shirley, you've been doing so many helpful things lately and doing them so well, I think you're ready to learn something new. I have three tasks in mind. Which one do you feel ready to try first? Setting the table for our dinner, maybe with candles and flowers to make it really nice; weeding the flower bed in the front yard, working on a small area each week; or would you rather learn to dust the living room with the pine-scented spray polish?" Vicky makes the jobs sound as attractive as possible, then lets her daughter make the final choice. Because Vicky knew what skills her daughter needed to develop, she could direct the goal, making sure to include the three teaching elements.

Shirley decided to weed the flower beds, so a piece of string was used to section off a four-foot square. When she had pulled the weeds within the string, her job was finished. Mother worked with Shirley for the first two Saturdays, to insure that flowers were not pulled with the weeds. After five weeks, the flower beds looked beautiful and needed only slight weeding each Saturday. Vicky told Shirley how lovely the flowers looked and what a fine job she was doing, occasionally working with her for a few minutes to make the job more enjoyable.

Let us suppose that you are setting goals for a ten-year-old boy. He does quite well with personal grooming and is willing to do little jobs, like setting the table and vacuuming, but his bedroom is a mess and he has expressed interest in cooking. The two basic goals are to help him get control of his bedroom and to learn some basic cooking skills. Set two or three short-range, specific goals that can be accomplished in about a month. The trick is to set workable tasks by asking, "What little things can be done to draw closer to these main goals?" The goals might be things like: -

Bedroom

• Make a progress chart for bed making and room pick-up.
• Give adult help once a week.
• Paint his bedroom.
• Move the sewing machine and fabrics out of his room.

Kitchen

• Make tuna fish sandwiches together.
• Prepare a lettuce salad with him.
• Direct him in making a cake from a mix.

As you discuss these goals, be sure to include the three teaching elements, so you and he both clearly understand what's expected, what is needed, and when he will do these things. Remember, this can be done formally on paper or informally in your discussion.

Continue setting goals. Most people set weekly and monthly goals at work, so why not at home? Now that you have a long-range goal of getting your children to work at home, you can set yearly and seasonal goals: "This summer I'll start teaching my daughter to sew." Include the child in these decisions. As adults, if we don't like something, we bag it. If we don't like singing, we don't sing in the choir. But children don't have the same privileges—they have to eat what is fixed for dinner, study the curriculum dictated by the school, and go to bed when parents say. If it's spelling they don't like, we tell them they need to work harder at it. These years can be difficult for the child. Whenever possible, allow the child to give as much input as is appropriate for his or her age.

Try to involve the child in setting individual goals. One father asks his children every Friday night, "What are your goals this weekend?" He says it has taken several months, but they have quit watching so much television and now are working on the things they "really" want to do. Talents are "interests" that have been nurtured; goal setting will help talents grow.

As you read this book, don't feel guilty because your kids aren't doing all you want them to do. There is no utopia, not even at the Monson or McCullough house. If you think our kids don't need prompting, don't procrastinate, or don't try to get out of work, you have the wrong impression. There is a time to crack down on laziness and carelessness. Sometimes we wonder what other people think when we tell them we're writing about getting children to work at home. These people have been in our homes when they were not clean, when we had to prompt our children to get busy. That's why there are so few books on this topic; most of those who write don't have kids and those who do have kids can't get them to work. By having a clear set of goals and working on them one at a time, we can stop worrying about everything at once. Goals cut down stress. But there are little moments when our children do things and we can see progress; like the first time Melea made a perfect sunny-side-up egg or when Wes said, "Let me wash the car for you, Mom." It's a good feeling when we go to parent-teacher conferences at school and the teachers say our children aren't afraid to speak in front of the class or that they are not fearful of new projects. Our children have not reached perfection, but they are not Annies either. This process of setting goals is fun and rewarding.

Children need much practice in each skill, sometimes even going back at a later point to relearn. Provide numerous opportunities: "I need to finish this painting before the storm hits, Charlie, so could you please make sandwiches for lunch?" They also need to learn to be consistent about a new responsibility. That's when a star chart or other means of visual feedback is helpful. Remember, the most important school your child will ever attend is your home. Give praise and encouragement freely, being grateful for small accomplishments. Self-esteem comes through finding a set of competencies. "Shirley, when you weed the flower beds, I feel like I have another woman helping me!" Listen as your child expresses feelings of frustration or success. Build on past successes, as you encourage them to meet future goals.

In a third grade classroom, the teacher taped a sign on the wall: "Hook your wagon to a star, take your seat and there you are." Goal setting is not quite that simple. Driving the team can be pretty hard work, but at least you have something by which to steer. Goal setting is the first step toward independence and responsibility. It will help make good times better and bad times better, too.

2: Knowing the Learning Seasons

WHEN TO TEACH THE PLAN

When is the best time to teach a particular skill? A child's learning stages can be divided into three seasons. The parents are the master teachers, with an opportunity to give the child the richest training he or she will ever use. Understanding the learning seasons helps them focus attention on a workable plan to productively use the 32,234 hours that a parent has to teach a child during the eighteen growing years at home. The three seasons of learning are:

1. Spring: ages two to five
2. Summer: ages five to twelve
3. Fall: ages thirteen to eighteen

SPRING—CONFIDENCE, OBEDIENCE, AND BASIC ROUTINE (2–5)

Typical of the first season is the "let me do it" stage of the preschooler. This is the time to lay the foundation of love, willingness, and confidence of "I can do something." Work is spontaneous and mostly voluntary. When the preschooler wants to help, encourage him by finding ways to let him feel helpful even though it may mean the job takes longer. If he wants to wash dishes, remove the glassware and sharp knives and let him. The reward for this patience will come when the child is older and you want him to work. Sarah Monson, almost two, watched Sue dust with an odd sock. Several days earlier they had visited the city art museum and had seen a display of the Sesame Street Muppets. It was not long before Sarah put the two experiences together, pushed her hand into the sock and said, "See my Dust Muppet." To capitalize on her creation, Sue drew a simple face on the sock with a marking pen. Sarah's confidence soared. It was a game to wipe the legs of the chairs, the top of the end table and the sides of the piano with her little muppet friend. Granted, she did not do all the dusting, but she did have a delightful, positive experience with helping. The groundwork was laid.

While building confidence, there is another important lesson for the preschooler to learn: *obedience.* Obedience comes from following through on realistic requests. When you say it is time to pick up the toys, then you have to see that the child does what you ask even though it often means interrupting a project and helping the child. Obedience can be taught. Even young children need to know that there are family rules. Tonya and Sally thought it was fun to take off their shoes and socks and run around barefoot. This was acceptable summer fun, but the growing-cold October days made it unreasonable. Even at two years of age, the girls could understand the new cold-weather rule: "If shoes and socks are taken off it is your choice, but you must go sit and play on the bed." It took two different offenses, two escorts to the bedroom, and being lifted upon the bed. The rule was understood. Several explanations were given the girls. They felt the cold floor and walls with their hands, they talked about the neighborhood swimming pool being closed, and they were reminded that sweaters and jackets were the usual apparel on these cooler days. Does all that sound like too much? It was not. Those words were not wasted because they were not scolding, threatening, or belittling as they often are when saying, "Get your shoes on right now or else." The careful follow-through helped the girls learn obedience. With insistence on obedience at this stage, the parent should understand the child does not visualize abstract concepts like "cold weather." She must be taught. This is a time for much loving patience. Know that the child will often need parental help to work and follow directions until six or seven years of age.

Next, the preschooler will start learning a *basic routine* of neatness, like making the bed and picking up toys, and a routine for personal grooming, like bathing, brushing teeth, and combing hair. Things that have to be done everyday. Another idea for encouraging the child to keep a basic routine is explained on page 84, Finger Plays for Chores.

SUMMER—TRAINING, SUCCESS, AND CONSISTENCY (5–12)

As the child moves into the Summer season at about age five, the apprenticeship begins to focus on:

1. Teaching the job

2. Fostering a feeling of success
3. Requiring consistent performance

The child continues working on the grooming and bedroom routines of Spring, but now is ready for specific training in household chores. You will find that children from age five to twelve are the best workers. The complexity of their jobs varies greatly during these seven years, but it is an important training period. After beginning junior high school, children get caught up in homework, sports, social activities, and self-identification with peer groups.

Basic training at age five is where the McCulloughs begin, when they introduce their children to a daily morning and evening chore. The child has the chore for a whole week, learning it well before moving on to another job. Success feelings come from keeping the learning steps small, making sure the three teaching elements (action, time and equipment, and standards) are met, providing many practice opportunities, and giving liberal praise. Consistent performance is required, and the child needs to experience natural or logical consequences if the job is not done. Regular checkups and follow-through are often necessary.

Mrs. Vincent provides us with an example of training, success feelings, and consistency of the Summer season that occurred when her son, Erin, neglected to water the dog. With a dramatic air she plopped ice cubes into the glasses on the dinner table. Her family was beginning to gather, and she made sure her actions were observed. Erin soon noticed his glass was empty. "Hey, Mom, you forgot to give me ice," he complained. Calmly Mom replied, "Oh, I thought since Barnie didn't have water in his bowl you didn't consider a drink very important." Mother was really saying, "Your job is to water the dog and you didn't." No more needed to be said. Erin quickly headed for the garage to water the dog. Using the time just prior to dinner was effective, because Erin had been trained to water the dog daily and the job took less than five minutes. While Erin watered the dog his glass was filled. When he returned, with the job completed, he had two immediate rewards—a feeling of acceptance and success. This is a one-time experience. A less cooperative child than Erin might refuse to water the dog right then. If so, simply follow through to the logical consequence of letting him go without a drink. For heightened impact, the child's favorite soft drink could be served to everyone else at this time.

As the children near their twelfth birthday, they are more on their own. They have experienced the success of learning many new skills, have done them on a regular basis with less and less supervision, have gained much confidence, and are ready to move into the Fall season.

FALL—INDEPENDENCE AND RESPONSIBILITY (13–18)

Fall arrives at about age thirteen with a splash of strong colors saying, "I can do it." Building on the growth from Spring and Summer, independence and responsibility play strong roles. Making use of this need for independence, guide and encourage your teenager to read how-to-books and manuals, to glean training for pre-occupational and adult skills. Let your teen-ager have a great deal to say about the selection of his or her goals, by going over the Home Progress Chart together. Much of the teen's life will be filled with school work, social activities, and self-identification with peer groups. This is as it should be, because those activities are an important part of maturing to adulthood. These children should also be more efficient in work techniques than the younger child. However, they still need some sort of regular housekeeping responsibility or they might learn the false assumption that "When you are busy, you have an excuse for not doing anything at home." There are many adults who conveniently fill their lives so full of outside activities that they excuse themselves from doing the less exciting routine housekeeping at home.

As you assess your child's needs and aptitudes, continue to make enjoyable opportunities available, such as music lessons, typing, woodworking, arts and crafts, sewing, or mechanical repairs, which will be helpful at home or work. Include meal planning and food selection. There might be surprises like cabbage salad instead of lettuce salad. Training should include opportunities to use and misuse money, through allowances and paid jobs. This is the time to systematically teach the various cleaning procedures, such as cleaning a stove top and oven. A sixteen-year-old can select one of the many oven cleaners on the market, read the instructions carefully, and proceed with the job. It is a good idea for a parent to be at home keeping an eye on the first attempt and offering help if needed. You may have wished, as do we, that the first oven you cleaned had been at home and not in your first apartment.

Because parent-teen communications are less than ideal at times, consider a grandparent, aunt, a respected adult, or another knowledgeable teen to teach some of the skills. It is surprising how much influence and direction you can have when you know your goals, even when getting someone else to help you accomplish them.

Sue found her teen children more willing to help after they heard an admired adult say, "My dad told me I had to help my mother with the dishes until I could out-run him. Dad was an excellent runner and I was sixteen before I beat him. But by then I was mature enough that I didn't mind helping with the dishes." Sue speculated that her children felt that if they complained about helping it would imply that they were less mature than they wanted to appear.

No teen will harvest every technique and skill to carry her through adulthood, but if she has learned enough to have confidence in her ability to learn more, and if she knows the essentials to survive, she will continue her learning progressions as an adult. We often give less encouragement at this age, because the teen expresses such strong desire for independence, but the teen still wants approval as much as anyone. After Maria, age fifteen, had done an especially good straightening job in the downstairs bathroom, Mom taped a note on the wall: "It was a pleasure to come into this room." After school the next day Maria complained, "Mom how come no note? I spent more time on the bathroom this morning than I did yesterday." We all like more pats on the back than we get; teen-agers are no exception.

SPRING, SUMMER, AND FALL

Usually the age at which you start does not matter, so long as you begin by teaching simple routines, then move on to chores that become more and more specific. There are too many varying circumstances to establish a strict guide. For instance, Annie at twenty needed to start basic cooking, a job another child might be doing at age eleven. At home, we need to be flexible and re-evaluate often for each child, making sure every skill agreed upon is necessary and, if it is, that a goal is set to achieve it. After developing through these three seasons, children should be prepared to face the storms and buffeting of the adult world.

BASIC HUMAN NEEDS

As parents we strive to satisfy the needs of our children. We feed them so they are not hungry, and provide shelter and clothing so they are safe from the elements. Most of our society is relatively free from tyranny and rampant crime: wild animals do not stalk us; and food is plentiful, although we may not be able to afford steak and delicacies at every meal. All in all, our physiological needs and safety needs are met, increasing the emphasis on the need to *belong* and the need to feel *esteem*. The need to belong means developing a sense of security, having a place and feeling a part of some larger group or plan. This includes satisfying the need to be needed. The esteem needs refer to the desire to be well thought of, having respect for oneself and recognition from others. Esteem needs can be broken down into the need to have

1. New experiences
2. Recognition
3. Opportunities to respond

The force our children can exert to meet the belonging and esteem needs can be very great, both through positive and negative actions. Many maladjustment cases are attributed to the lack of meeting the belonging and esteem needs. We do not attempt in this book to deal with maladjustment or any serious psychological or social problems that can surface in a family. Such problems require outside help and professional counseling.

We do believe, however, that the process of preparing your child for the adult world, training and allowing him or her to have many and varied experiences in helping at home, can do much to satisfy the belonging and esteem needs. It is nice to feel like you belong. A twelve-year-old boy stated, "Children should help at home because it's our house and we should all help to take care of it." These expressions of feeling a part of a family appeared often in our survey of 250 children. In the rushed pace of today's world, with mothers and fathers both working, children shuffling from one lesson to another, and with demands of community and school activities, children sense the real need for their help at home. Participation by children makes them feel a vibrant, necessary member of the family.

The esteem need of having new experiences can be gratified each time the child is taught a new skill. The regularity and variety of jobs around the home is endless. For instance, meal planning and cooking can lead from a boiled egg to a gourmet omelet. Instant recognition for the child's help can be given through using abundant positive statements, charts, and games. Praise can be given for real achievement, as the child sees regular growth on the Home Progress Chart. Use of the planning sessions in family council provides opportunity for the child to offer suggestions and register complaints. These things help fill the need to respond. A sense of security will come from learning new skills. The time you invest in being with your child to build these skills and in praising efforts as discussed in this book will be time well spent.

After the sudden and untimely death of an American woman living in Germany, her friends paid tribute by observing, "If any children can survive this tragedy, these five children can because their mother prepared them well." Will your children be so lucky?

3: Getting the Family Together

Now that you have set your goals, what is the next step? To get the children's cooperation and commitment. The family council is an ideal vehicle for accomplishing this. It can be a spontaneous sharing of ideas that no one recognizes as a meeting, or it can be like a formal "board of directors" meeting that assembles every week to discuss family business. The family council can

1. Contribute to each member's sense of belonging
2. Develop a structure of rules and policies so each member

will understand the boundaries and individual
responsibilities
3. Provide experience in problem solving, negotiating,
and compromise
4. Allow each member an opportunity to respond by
contributing ideas and suggesting solutions
5. Facilitate the goal-setting and achievement process
6. Foster individual commitment and increased
cooperation
7. Provide practice in leadership
8. Share desires and concerns of family members
9. Develop the security of consistency, oneness, and
fairness

SETTING UP A FAMILY COUNCIL

How do you set up a family council? The basic structure
could be like a committee, with the father and mother (if two-
parent family) as cochairpersons and the children as board
members. Each member could have a vote, but the parents re-
tain the veto power. Discussions should be handled with the
same courtesy that would be shown good friends, with each
member having opportunities to initiate ideas, actions, and solutions. Brainstorm, remaining open to all suggestions, and
hold off decisions until the whole issue has been presented.
These techniques can foster unity rather than the room-and-
board life style of uncommitted families. But, don't expect a
hundred percent success. The meeting will probably even dete-
riorate into an argument once in a while.

When will council be held?   Depending on your circumstances, it could be held one evening after dinner, early Saturday morning, or Sunday afternoon; once a month or every
week. The small family with very young children probably
won't be having as many relationship and calendar problems
as the family with older children, when rides and schedules get

so complicated, but the sooner you start the habit of open family discussion, the better it will work later. Keep the meeting short. The length of time has a direct bearing on its success. Most business can be handled in fifteen minutes; after thirty minutes the efficiency drops. It would be better to have weekly twenty-minute councils than one monthly two-hour session!

How will it be used? Some parents use the family council not only as a family business meeting, but also as a time for instruction and play. Parents could teach their children safety, manners, social relations, and moral concepts, in which case the family meeting would take longer. It could be a time for carving a pumpkin, making holiday decorations, planting a garden, or learning to sew on buttons. There are many possibilities with this family council; often it becomes a family evening together. Can you picture your family all staying home together at the same time? It doesn't just happen; it has to be planned and guarded, or other things will interfere. Statistics from the former U.S. Department of Health, Education and Welfare indicate that by holding a regular family gathering one hour a week, whether it be for fun, talk, or formal instruction, you reduce the probability of your child having serious problems with delinquency, alcohol, drugs, and so forth by up to forty-two percent. Parents who make such an effort realize that if they don't plan the time now, the days will slip by and the children will be grown. One trick for making it successful is to have refreshments after the meeting, which gives someone the opportunity to practice cooking skills, too.

When an unpredicted problem or opportunity comes up, a special family meeting could be called. The Sworts family always has a planning meeting the first day of summer vacation to map out activities, set goals, and talk about work assignments. They also hold a council meeting in November to organize their Christmas activities. For instance, they vote on when the tree should be put up. Mrs. Sworts was brought up in a home where the tree was decorated the night before Christmas and left up until New Year's Day, but her children would rather enjoy it several weeks before Christmas. The Sworts children are allowed the fun of developing their own traditions. Their council also decides on a service project to be carried out and the goodies to be given friends and teachers. At the same time their children are learning independence, they are also learning cooperation and have achieved a healthy but mutual dependency within the family.

Make an effort to grow your own family traditions. They provide definite times to get together, give family life a general framework, and endow the family with its own unique complexion. Holidays and birthdays are prime times for family customs ranging from the strategy you use when decorating the Christmas tree to buying Easter seals. Traditions can be saying "sweet dreams" at bedtime, sleeping in on Saturday morning, trick-or-treating on Halloween, the birthday person picking the dinner menu, visiting the cemetery on Memorial Day, or popping corn on Sunday night. Use some traditions inherited from your youth and develop others with your own children. Family council is a good place to talk about new ideas. Make time to be together. Sometimes this means we have to learn to do an activity that is not first choice. It may be learning to fish, camp, ride a bicycle, or even play baseball. Families can be fun.

What will be talked about?   Start by asking each individual family member if they have any family business to discuss. If they know this opportunity will be available at each meeting, they will begin thinking about it ahead of time and bring up such things as: "Can I bring home the hamster from our school classroom this weekend?" "Little brother keeps getting into my room." "What can we do about dirty clothes left under the bed?" This is where parents have to help manage the discussion and not let it be destructive. Keep it positive. It is a time to problem-solve, negotiate, and compromise. A mediocre solution with everyone's approval is better than a superior solution ramrodded by an adult or a persuasive teenager. Let the children learn from this process; don't dictate all the actions.

When the child says, "It isn't fair," listen. It means he cares, but something isn't quite right and some correction may need to be made. It might be appropriate at this meeting to ask some positive questions like "What did you like best about your weekend?" to point out good accomplishments or events. Parents could rotate giving the children opportunities to conduct this meeting, and an appointed secretary could record topics discussed. This way you can measure progress at the next meeting.

This is a good time to openly discuss problems. If given a chance, children can often come up with very logical or ingenious solutions because they are not as locked into traditional thought patterns. Let the ideas flow freely. In our survey, when children were asked what would make their jobs easier they said it would help "if I knew ahead of time what I was supposed to do so I could do the work at my own time, like during boring TV shows." Another child said, "it would help if people cleaned up after themselves." One boy reported that more trash cans would make his job easier. Children will also have some out-of-reach ideas like getting a riding lawn mower or a maid. Part of the experience is learning they can't have everything they want. Allowances might be paid at this time, special budget items could be mentioned, or a vacation planned. Your aim should be to teach children that there is more than one way to solve a problem. Parents must realize that the solutions to problems may be a little different than if they make the decisions alone. The reward is that when children feel they have a part in the decision they are more likely to cooperate.

An important part of family council is coordinating schedules and responsibilities. Talk about work times, meetings, baby-sitting assignments, needed rides, music or talent lessons, birthday parties, and all the other activities of family members. This way everyone will have advance notice of upcoming commitments and be saved from last-minute surprises like "Oh, I need eight dozen cookies by three o'clock." Don't forget to talk about who will make the cupcakes to take to the meeting, or when you will go shopping for that birthday gift, and maybe who will pay for it.

If your family is involved in many activities, or battles irregular schedules, a family planning calendar is essential. Ideally, it will be large enough to write commitments in the date boxes and will be posted where everyone will see it often—possibly in the kitchen by the telephone. Update this calendar at least once a week and make other entries as they come up. When notices come home from school for parent-teacher conferences or class pictures, make a note on the calendar. This means you can throw away most of the stack of such notices. As party invitations or wedding announcements arrive, pencil them in. If you have the space, a bulletin board around the calendar gives you a place to keep the invitations until the event has passed. Besides using the family planning calendar, the Cooper family has devised a method of using colored markers to write in their commitments, so family members can tell at a glance if the entry concerns them. A red marker is used to designate activities that affect the whole family, green initials for the kids, brown for Mom and blue for Dad.

Another way to get organized is for family members to have their own calendar date book and to update it at family council. This will cost a little more, but in families with older children it may be more effective.

The Family Activity Schedule gives a visual view of family activities for the entire year. It helps family members include worthwhile activities but avoid overscheduling. The Monsons use the Family Activity Schedule to jog their memory of cultural events, museum or zoo visits, and family birthdays. It is so easy to let the months fly by without doing what you really want to do. Patterns of heavy commitments or uneven time investments can be promptly changed. If three members of your family have birthdays in July, don't schedule a garage sale in July. If May is a busy month with yard preparations and school programs, it may not be a good time to start an evening class or take a vacation. Maybe your family decides to have a monthly outing, either dining out, going to a movie, or visiting a museum. By having the Family Activity Schedule in front of you, it is easier to add a greater variety of activities and include the different interests of family members. The overall yearly scheduling could be done in January and July, and the deciding of the specific times to do an activity at the beginning of each month. (See page 38 for a sample schedule.)

ESTABLISHING THE RULES

Another purpose of the family council is to discuss rules and policies. At one of their regular meetings, the Anderson family decided to write down family rules in the form of a bill of rights. They review the rules and add or change them when needed.

Keep such a list simple and positive, saying things like "keep toys picked up" rather than "don't leave toys out." Stress the desired behavior. Having too many rules dampens their effectiveness. You might brainstorm a long list of rules and then vote on the most important ones, keeping it to fewer than fifteen rules. Many rules are unspoken; they are just a part of your style of living. These unspoken standards are sometimes very noticeable when outsiders come to play at your home and, for instance, they take the scissors out to the sand box or use felt-tip markers in the living room. When your children understand the rule, they will say to their friends, "At our house we don't do that."

Find and use good ideas from different sources. For instance, good business techniques can be used at home, but don't be like the father in *The Sound of Music,* who ran his house with the rules and structure of a ship and neglected understanding. A department store could not function without some sort of system like assigning employees to various departments and describing their duties. Some families leave it to happenstance. Make good use of planning and management principles, but with the love and intimacy applicable to the family unit.

ANDERSON BILL OF RIGHTS AND RESPONSIBILITIES

1. We each have the right to our toys, books, and clothes. Others should ask before borrowing them.

2. We will each be responsible for our own bedroom area and two other household chores a day.

3. Everyone will help with dinner dishes and, except for special occasions, no one is excused until the kitchen is clean.

4. We will eat food *only* in the kitchen and dining areas, to preserve furniture and carpets not designed for easy clean-up of juicy or greasy foods.

5. We will be dressed, and our beds will be made each morning *before* breakfast.

6. We are responsible for putting our own things (coats, books, toys, projects) away, out of consideration for other family members.

7. If delayed, we will call home to explain, so others won't worry.

8. We will speak kindly to each other and about each other.

9. After using something, we will put it away where it belongs, even if that isn't where we found it.

AGREEING ON HOUSEHOLD STANDARDS

It will help the parents if the children are part of a decision as to what is an acceptable level of housekeeping and if they understand why their help is expected. Remember, people are more important than things, but the order of things affects people. A filthy house is unhealthful, a cluttered house slows down everything you try to do, and a sterile house takes too much time to get it that way. In a tidy home, every task is easier and people feel better about themselves, but you don't have to devote your life to cleaning.

In your neighborhood you probably live under a set of covenants that govern such things as the cleanliness of your yard, how many and what kind of animals you can keep, and the placement of buildings, even though the property is yours. As a family, talk about and agree on the rules of maintenance for the general family living areas: kitchen, living room, family room, stairs, and entries. If one person leaves the living room a mess, it affects other family members. Agree on a household standard. Part of this agreement should be deciding on the purpose and use of the various rooms. You may decide some rooms are for show, some for gathering, some for quiet study, and some for work. Using the right rooms for their designed purposes will keep the paraphernalia from working, cooking, and playing contained in the areas that are built for easy clean up and storage.

"Learning how to work step-by-step through a chore helps children apply the same principles in their own work and play," stated Harris Clemes, Ph.D., and Reynold Bean, E.M., in their book *How To Teach Children Responsibility.* They also say, "Learning to keep things organized results from having experienced things being organized. When a child participates physically, mentally and emotionally, in the organization of things within the home, his capability to do so in school and in other activities will be immeasurably increased." Clemes and Bean go on to say, "Dealing with 'external tasks' helps chil-

FAMILY ACTIVITY SCHEDULE

Activity	Jan.	Feb.	Mar.	April	May	June	July	Aug.	Sept.	Oct.	Nov.	Dec.
Family Outing	Museum	Movie	Pizza	Movie	Picnic on Mt.	Zoo						
Birthdays		New Baby					Melissa Sarah	Dave		Eric	Sue	
Garage Sale						✓						
Grandparents Visit				2nd week								
Clean Yard Trim Trees					✓							
Major House Cleaning						✓						
Plant Garden				✓	✓	✓						
School Sewing							✓	✓				
Vacation							✓					

dren to organize their 'internal processes.' Even growth in logical thinking is aided by learning the 'logic' of ordinary household procedures such as putting toys away or cleaning one's room. Furthermore, being required to do chores helps children learn to deal with frustration and ambiguity. Children who do chores regularly become better problem solvers."

As a family, talk about how you want your home to look, then set up assignments. The next several chapters discuss ways to teach your children to work, letting them know exactly what is expected and making assignments with chore charts, then following up. Don't get the idea we are going to tell you how to get your children to do *all* the work, all the time. It is as unfair to ask children to do all the housework as it is to expect the parents to do all the housework.

HOLDING PERSONAL INTERVIEWS

Although some problems are discussed in a council, others should be handled privately. A few parents take their child aside, perhaps into the den, once a month for a formal interview to discuss problems, set goals, and talk about feelings. Other parents do the same thing less formally, by making one-to-one opportunities while riding in the car with the radio off or taking the child for an ice-cream cone and asking a few leading questions and then just listening. Parents of very young children find it easy to take a minute to talk with the child at bedtime. Asking questions "What was the nicest thing that happened to you today?" or "What did you do for someone else?" will help foster a positive outlook and develop a closer parent-child relationship.

"We want it to be fair," children say. It is possible to treat each child fairly, but not the same. They are not identical, for each one is different even if they happen to be twins. Try and make some distinctions by age or interests. For example, allowances could be paid at the rate of so much per year of age.

Bedtime could be structured so that the younger child goes to bed fifteen minutes before the older one. Some families have rules like "Makeup for girls only after reaching junior high school," or "No single dating until age sixteen." Each child wants to feel he or she is important and has his or her own identity, and different age privileges can help that. Also, watching for their differences in learning styles, needs, talents, and ambitions can help you recognize these distinctions among your children. Each child wants to feel his or her place in the family is unique.

Discouraging figures were quoted by Dr. Stephen Glenn during a lecture to educators. "In the United States," he said, "the average child over ten years of age (in a two-parent home) has fourteen and a half minutes interaction with his parents in twenty-four hours. Twelve minutes of this time is spent issuing warnings or correcting things that have gone wrong, leaving only about two minutes of 'open' time per day or twelve to fourteen minutes per week of individual communication time. This would include collaborative activities, even working together, but not watching TV. Most families don't even eat together." This average is so low, it would be easy to increase parent-child time by one hundred percent just by eating dinner together (activities don't have to be one to one). You could read a book with your children, help them wash the dishes, pull weeds, or clean their bedroom together and be well above the national average. Your children need your presence more than your presents.

CREATING ORDER THROUGH ROUTINE

A by-product of the family council is a feeling of consistency. Mutual understanding of basic rules and rights and common goals are important elements of consistency and they bring about unity. A second part of consistency is order. A routine need not look like a bus schedule, but should have enough order to give the family a rhythm around which other activities can be built. The only thing some people do every day is eat, and often this is on the run. A simple family schedule gives a sense of security and helps establish consistency by setting a time to do other things such as dressing, eating, playing, dishes, homework, and so forth. The Thompson family is an appropriate example. Though a large family of six, the children's interests and talents were always first. They were involved in dance lessons, a drama club, soccer, basketball, Cub Scouts, and Boy Scouts just to mention a few. Mr. Thompson was a self-employed salesman; his work hours were sporadic and he often worked evenings. Mrs. Thompson, though totally

devoted to her family, was stretched beyond her emotional limits. The psychologist told this family the first thing to do would be to set a time for dinner, within a one-hour span (such as five-thirty to six-thirty), in which dinner would be served every day. Even if Dad couldn't be there, the children and Mom needed that time of day as a central pivot on which to line up their lives. The Thompsons were told to cut back on activities so this dinner hour could be possible. They had been concentrating so heavily on developing talents that there wasn't time for the heartbeat of routine and they were losing their bearings.

We all avoid work if we can, and one way of avoiding work is to fill our lives so full of other things that we have an excuse for not doing the dishes or cleaning our rooms. Eventually this backfires because when you can't get someone else to do these daily upkeep jobs, they get in the way and block doing anything else. The theory, then, is to teach the children to handle the basics with efficiency so they have a strong foundation to build on for other things. The Thompsons found that a simple routine with breakfast and dinner at regular times was very therapeutic in helping Mom's depression and still allowed for a few other activities.

A family routine should set aside certain times to do specific things. For example, when you set early morning as the time that the beds will be made and everyone dressed, then you are free from worrying about those for the rest of the day. You would be surprised at the number of people who don't even brush their teeth every day. When should bedtime be? When will you eat breakfast? Your answer might be that breakfast is generally about seven, but not until nine on Saturday. Maybe your Saturdays are set aside for projects, catch-up jobs and fun, and Sunday is your day off. These are the beginnings of a family routine. A schedule makes it easier to "hook on" new habits. It's easy to say "Your time to practice piano will be from seven to seven-thirty, right after breakfast" when breakfast is served regularly at about the same time. Otherwise, there is uncertainty and a new time for practice has to be "found" every day. There should also be a schedule for weekends, although slightly relaxed, to include such things as making the bed and daily pick-up. It's interesting to note that most suicides are on the weekends and holidays, when people aren't committed to do something. Keep the schedule flexible but firm enough to give a basic structure to your life. A simple routine is like putting gelatin powder in water: After setting, it holds the liquid in a form that doesn't run all over.

After deciding you want your children to be independent and still do some work at home, you must get their cooperation. If cooperation is a problem in your home, getting together as a family and privately to set goals and discuss rules will help. Involve them in framing the structure of your family rules and policies through family communication. The whole reasoning behind this family council is to satisfy the needs to be listened to, to participate and to respond, and to feel your ideas are valid. Serving on a family council is good experience; it may well prepare your children to be more effective in school and business. It gives a vehicle to pull it all together. A non-functioning committee is useless. Get yours moving.

4: Assigning the Job with Charts

Charts are fun and functional. From the children's work survey, we found that the majority of parents just *tell* their children which jobs to do. This puts the parent in the *telling* position and the child in the *doing* category. If the parent doesn't *tell*, the child doesn't *do*. The chore chart is a fantastic tool for pulling the parent away from *telling*, making the chart the regulator, getting some of the emotion out of the situation and strengthening both independence and responsibility.

The best advantage to chore charts is that they indicate *what is expected*. It is important to lay a careful foundation *before*

THE ADVANTAGES OF CHORE CHARTS

* Chore charts can add *variety* and interest to otherwise drab work.
* A feeling of *fairness* is created by letting the child know his assignments ahead of time.
* They aid *order* by expecting every child to take a share of the household work every day as part of family membership.
* Chore charts *rotate assignments* so the child develops more skills than just setting the table and emptying the trash.
* Chore charts can give immediate *positive rewards* for accomplishments.
* They *cut down* sibling *rivalry* because the children understand everyone will have a turn at every job.

---

declaring, "It is work time." Much of your success at teaching your child to work is dependent on laying this groundwork first: setting goals and family rules, teaching proper work techniques, and assigning the work with chore charts. All of these increase the chances of getting the child to work. After the assignment has been made, the parent needs to teach the child *how* to do a job, which is explained in Chapter Five. (Show and Tell step-by-step p. 72)

In this chapter, we will offer twenty-four charts for your selection. These twenty-four charts are divided into three types. The first type, Assignment Charts, set up a stable routine and give the child advance notice of assignments. The second type, Fun and Challenge Charts, are used to counter the complaint that "housework is so boring." The third type, Progress Charts, offer more ideas designed to keep track of daily accomplishments and to positively reward a desired habit. Use these ideas or create charts of your own. In the beginning it will take more time to teach your children to work than if you simply did it yourself; but in the end, you will have more time to do other things with them. It's worth the effort.

Chore charts aid consistency. So many books say, "Be consistent, consistent, consistent." How can I teach my child to be consistent when *I* am not consistent? Are you assuming that consistency means a regular routine, performing the same things every day—everyone making their bed every day, everyone doing all their chores, everyone picking up all their belongings, and the parents checking the kids' bedrooms every day before they leave for school? Most of us feel like failures because we are not consistent in that way. On the other hand, we all know parents whose children have turned out to be successful, independent, and responsible who didn't do all those things. Consistency is knowing what is expected, knowing what the task is, knowing a reward will be given if one was promised, knowing that wrong choices reap the logical consequences. This is consistency in principle. Chore charts can help you establish this regularity. However, sometimes we confuse consistency with sameness, which it is not. Consistency is not a minute-by-minute routine. Consistency is not putting everything away the minute you walk into the house. That is perfection. If we were to do the same thing the same way every day, we would be so inflexible we would be unhappy.

The foundation of consistency is built by meeting the basic security needs of food, clothing, and warmth. Give yourself credit for providing those things. It is impossible to be consistent in every detail, but you are probably consistent with basic principles. The feeling of unity, fairness, cooperation, understanding, acceptance, and love give stability and security to the child. Children receive security from knowing family and household rules and knowing goal expectations, the topics already discussed in the first three chapters.

Consistency is reinforced with orderliness. The remainder of this book deals mostly with achieving consistency through order, but with fun. Childhood can be a powerless time. The child wants to know what to expect. This kind of consistency is a treasure. Even though the job is not more important than a child, there is a need for basic order—it gives rhythm, it provides a place for certain tasks, and saves confusion. Some things should not be skipped—basics like brushing teeth and eating. Because we eat, we have to cook and wash dishes. Being consistent in principle, with love and understanding, means you can be flexible with the *process*. Because you know that people are more important than things, and because things and schedules sometimes need to be changed to accommodate people, you change the ways and means. For example at some stages it is better to wash dishes in teams and at other times it may be better to divide the task up into individual assignments. There may even be times when one person is excused from dishes. The principle is the same—the dishes must be washed—but the way it is done can be changed. Changing the method may take the dullness out of washing the dishes.

We can also change the work process for variety. According to Robert L. DeBruyn, using variety does not destroy consistency; it actually has nothing to do with order. Imagination, change, and variety are the ingredients that "heighten the appetite for learning." Boredom may inadvertently become the condition in your home out of your efforts to be consistent if there is too much routine. Dullness comes out of using the same method to achieve the task, not out of doing the job. For example, if your goal is for the child to learn to take care of the bedroom, the goal will remain the same, but the teaching techniques, methods of inspection, and incentives may vary greatly over the years.

Consistency doesn't mean a bedroom has to pass a fifty-point inspection every day. As adults, we do not work in the house the same amount of time every day because higher priorities come up. Give the child the same kind of understanding. Consistency for the bedroom could be "It needs to be orderly most of the time, cleaned well on the weekend or once a month." On the other hand, it is a defeating work habit to entirely neglect the minimum necessities of grooming and pick-up. Self-image reflects one's environment. Even small regular jobs, assigned and rewarded by chore charts, will help maintain a balance between perfection and mess. The purpose of this book is to offer many ideas to spark up family life and to set a tone of consistency in principle and consistency in orderliness so the child will be prepared to face the Big World.

As the child gets older, you will want to adjust the chores, change your requirements, and include him or her in your decision making. Whatever work patterns you choose for your children will naturally have to fit your own pattern, whether it be very structured or relaxed.

ASSIGNMENT CHARTS

Vertical chore chart. The McCullough family has used a simple vertical chore chart for the last ten years to assign the children their jobs. The children like it, because they know ahead of time exactly what their chore will be and, especially during the Summer season (years five to twelve), they have had the job long enough to learn it well and reap the time-saving reward of efficiency.

The chore chart has two rows of pockets; the first one for morning and the second for evening. Every Monday morning the chores are rotated. Before assigning the chores, Bonnie looked around for areas of the home that needed daily care and determined what tasks the children could complete in less than ten minutes (their time) without being dependent on someone else's performance first. As it came out, the morning chores were the minimum maintenance (pick-up) for the main living areas of the home. The evening chores centered around dinner preparation, because everyone already helped with clean-up after dinner.

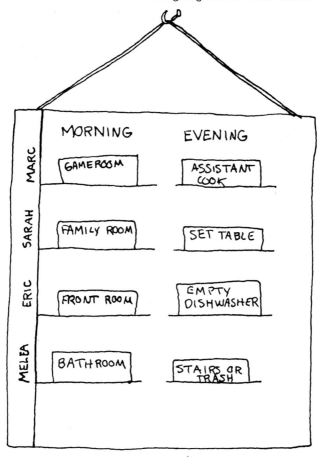

Although every child gets a chance in each area, the expectations change according to the age, keeping the requirements within the child's ability. For example: When the five-year-old cleans the bathroom, he only scours the sink, shakes the rug, and puts away the combs and toothbrushes. When the fifteen-year-old cleans the bathroom, she is expected to clean the bathtub, the toilet, and the floor, also.

Having a regular time every day for this work helps get it done, and we do want them to succeed at their assignments. Some days it is only a light pick-up, other days it is a thorough

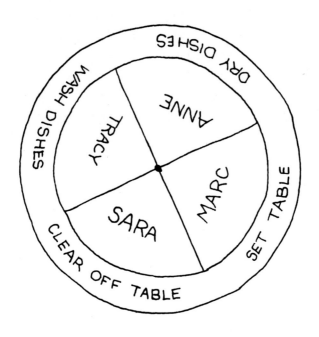

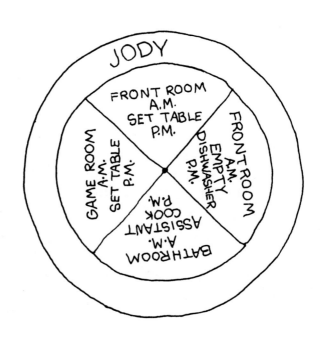

cleaning. When the children were all in grade school, these chores were done every morning before school. In the summer they were done before 10 A.M., and every evening at 5 P.M. However, now that the older McCullough children are advancing into the Fall season (years thirteen to eighteen), and are leaving for school as early as 5:45 A.M., the before-school requirements have been modified and the daily pick-up is done before dinner. They have also switched to a two-hour, Saturday morning cleaning schedule, where they thoroughly clean their own bedrooms and assigned-chore room, leaving the weekdays to concentrate on school homework. It is important to adjust the chores, change the requirements, and include the children in the decision-making process as they mature.

Circular chore chart. There are hundreds of possibilities for the chore charts to fit varying family circumstances. For a one- or two-child family, where the children have equal ability, perhaps a circular chore chart would be best. Naturally, you will not expect them to do all ten jobs the McCullough kids do, because there are fewer of them; but then your child should get to do more than empty the trash and wash dishes. This chart will rotate jobs and give variety. To adapt the chart to fit the quantity of work and number of workers, simply make a different number of pie-shaped divisions on the chart. Two circles, one smaller than the other, are cut from heavy paper. Use a thumbtack or brad in the center so the circles can be turned separately. Post it where it can be easily seen, such as in the kitchen.

Flag in a cup. Since some jobs don't need to be done every day, you might prefer to make assignments according to what needs to be done. The job could be written on a three-by-five card and slipped into the child's slot in a job box every morning, or little flags made on popsicle sticks could be set in cups to show the day's assignments. One of the drawbacks of this system is that kids cannot start to work until the parents put out the cards or flags. Sometimes it is hard to be that organized each morning.

The floor plan. Another possible way to assign cleaning responsibilities might be by drawing a floor plan of your house, either on fabric (in which case you could frame it), or on paper, so it could be posted on the refrigerator. Put a picture of the person in the room he or she is responsible for cleaning. This will not work for separate jobs like taking out the trash or drying the dishes, but it could be used when work is assigned by territory. (Mom and Dad could be included in this.)

Daily assignment chart. One single parent, father of three, ran off a stack of the following daily assignment charts at a quick-copy shop. Each night he and his children filled in the assignments for the next day and posted them on the refrigerator. His reason for changing the assignments every day was to coordinate chores with the children's heavy homework and activities. Besides, not every chore needs to be done every day. This chart allowed for volunteers and could include Dad. Charts like this might also be filled out for the whole week at the family council meeting.

Monthly calendar chart. When asked if his family used an assignment chart, one boy wrote, "We go by the calendar for dishes. My brothers and I do them every three days." A girl wrote, "My sister and I fight about whose turn it is to feed the dog, so we use the calendar and put our initials on every other

DAILY ASSIGNMENT CHART

Saturday
_____
Day of week

Breakfast
Cook _James_
Set Table _Stephanie_
Clear Dishes _Dad_

Lunch
Cook _Stephanie_
Set Table _Heather_
Clear Dishes _Dad_

Dinner
Cook _Dad_
Set Table _James_
Clear Dishes _Stephanie_

Room Assignments
Upstairs Bathroom _Heather_
Downstairs Bathroom _Stephanie_
Living Room _Dad_
Entry _James_

Other Assignments
Empty Dishwasher _Heather_
Trash _James_

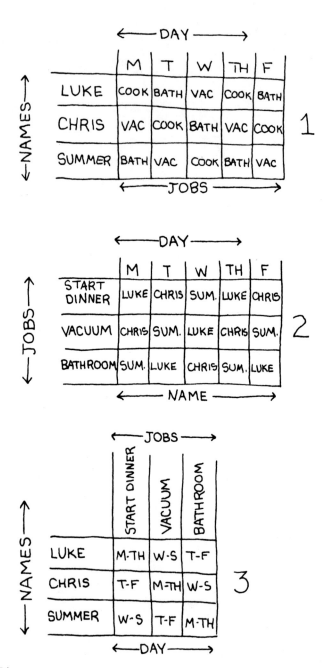

space so we know whose turn it is." With this method, you write the child's first initial in the calendar box, filling in the whole month. When the child completes the job, he or she crosses it off. If a trade-off is made, it could save misunderstandings for tomorrow if it were recorded on the assignment calendar. If activities and appointments are also written on the calendar, lighter assignments could be given to the busier person.

Weekly assignment charts. The family's assignments for an entire week can be shown on one chart. These weekly assignment charts have three categories: day, child, and assignment. A chart can be designed in several different ways, but it must have the same basic grid, with one of the three categories across the top, another down the side, and the third in the boxes between. This chart could be made on poster board and covered with clear contact paper and written on with a washable marking pen.

One working mother also posts menus in the daily square of the assignment chart, because she expects her older children to have dinner well under way by the time she gets home from work. Making the dinner decision early, especially for working parents, takes off a lot of pressure after work. If dinner is planned, other family members are more likely to help.

Another parent, even though she only has one child, writes out her fifteen-year-old daughter's assignments this way:

	M	T	W	TH	F
MARY	Vacuum	Clean Bathroom	Clean Kitchen	Clean Bedroom	Dust Wash Floor

Kathie Liden had the suggestion of using cup hooks to make a permanent assignment chart by screwing various chore markers into a board. Markers can be round key tags, squares of wood, or cardboard shapes. The shapes could represent a fa-

vorite family activity (like a soccer ball for a family who plays soccer), a pet or mascot. The jobs are written on the shape and arranged as assigned. This chart may have one drawback, in that it might suggest itself to one child to secretly trade disagreeable chores with another. Rules against this would have to be made up beforehand.

The helping hand. Create your own chart known as Mother's Helping Hand by cutting a hand shape out of wood or cardboard, or by stuffing an old formal glove, or by sewing an arm from a strip of calico. The hand and fingers could be shaped from an old nylon stocking. Put hooks on the bottom for jobs. When the task is finished, the marker could be moved from the assignment hook and hung from the fingers or from a fancy ring.

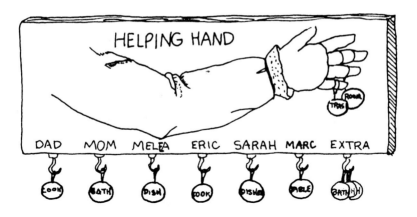

FUN AND CHALLENGING METHODS

Chance assignments. On Saturday, the Troxell family writes the chores to be done on little slips of paper and puts them in a jar, then each family member (including Mom and Dad) draws out his/her assignment. They work hard on Saturday morning, leaving the afternoon for fun or personal projects.

To adapt this idea to different circumstances, the jobs could be for one day, or for the rest of the week. Anything could be used to hold the chore slips: hat, plastic pumpkin, or Easter basket. You could number the jobs and roll dice to see which one is yours, or just pick them out of someone's hand like cards. Sometimes a little variety perks up the attitude toward work.

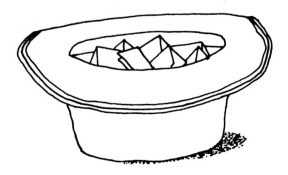

Choose a job. At times it is more rewarding and gives extra incentive for the child to *choose* the job. One Saturday morning when unexpected company was announced, Sue Monson was in a bind to get all the work done. She called her two older children together and explained that the work would take five hours to do. No one had five hours that day, but if they all worked for one and a half hours everything could be finished before Uncle Darold and Aunt Kathy arrived. "Here is the list of things that need to be done. Let's take turns choosing jobs from the list. Eric chooses one job first, Melea next, me next, and then we will start with Eric again." Sharing the work among several family members makes it seem easier. Dividing these jobs into five- and ten- and fifteen-minute projects makes them look attainable and gives immediate rewards of completion. Another parent used the same idea, but put the jobs on three-by-five cards so that each child had his own little stack, and they turned each card in to Dad as tasks were finished so he could inspect. Monson's emergency list for getting ready for company looked like this:

BUSY DAY CHECK LIST

Estimated Time:	Must Do:	Who Will Do It?
30 min.	Mow front lawn	_____
30 min.	Mow back lawn	_____
15 min.	Trim along sidewalk	_____
10 min.	Sweep patio and steps	_____
10 min.	Hose off patio and steps	_____
15 min.	Vacuum basement stairs	_____
30 min.	Dishes, noon and evening	_____
10 min.	Sweep kitchen floor	_____
20 min.	Mop kitchen floor	_____
30 min.	Make cake	_____
15 min.	Vacuum living room and hall	_____
10 min.	Dust living room	_____
5 min.	Clean toilet	_____
5 min.	Sweep bathroom floor	_____
10 min.	Damp-mop bathroom floor and wipe off woodwork	_____
10 min.	Shake all upstairs throw rugs	_____
15 min.	Change linen in guest bedroom	_____
10 min.	Vacuum guest bedroom	_____
10 min.	Dust guest bedroom	_____
20 min.	Cut and arrange fresh flowers	_____

Lists. Children love to have a list of their jobs for the day, especially on no-school days, when they do not have the "tardy" consequence to make them hurry. They feel satisfied as they cross off each item, but the biggest reward is in knowing that when this list is all marked off, they are *finished* and the rest of the day is theirs. The young child feels he is really making progress as he marks off even the basics of brushing teeth and hair. Once the habit is formed of doing the basic grooming and dressing, those details need not be included on the list.

Contract. A written contract with the child is a two-way commitment rather than just the one-sided *telling*. It is okay if it's the parent's idea, but even better when the child agrees. The reward for doing the job on time and consequences for not meeting the deadline could be stated in the contract. This contract agreement can be for a one-time job, like cleaning the garage, or for a regular job habit, like setting the table on time for one week. The reward could be money, special time with the parent, or a trade-off in labor. Use your imagination.

SAMPLE CONTRACT

December
Date to be done

*ride in car to
deliver Wednesday
paper route*
Reward to be given

I *Trevor* _____ contract to clean my room, which includes picking up the floor clutter, cleaning off the desk, dresser, and end table, making my bed, dusting the furniture, and sweeping the floor.

Trevor Atkinson
worker

Pat Atkinson
employer

PROGRESS CHARTS

There are times when a daily chart can be used to show accomplishment and give immediate reinforcement. These can be used when trying to promote basic follow-through, such as helping very young children to make beds or brush teeth. Such charts are successful even with older children as a perk-up when there has been a letdown on daily responsibilities. Sometimes, when working on a habit change, an incentive chart like these can help motivation. The following charts can be made so that the child can reward himself immediately without the parent always being directly involved. (Check Chapter Seven, page 103, for even more incentives.)

Star chart. The simple daily Star Chart is a terrific motivator, especially for the young child who is learning basic skills like personal grooming and room care. It works, too, for older children who need a little boost with their consistency. A progress chart is especially helpful at the beginning of summer, when kids are tempted to let down totally without the struc-

STAR CHART

NANCY

Morning Routine before 10 A.M.	M	T	W	TH	F	S	S
Teeth	★				★		
Hair	★	★	★	★	★		
Bed	★	★	★		★		
Dressed	★	★	★	★	★		
Toys	★		★		★		

PROGRESS CHART FOR OLDER CHILDREN

		M	T	W	TH	F	S	S
JODIE	Room	✓	✓	✓	0	✓	✓	
	Music Practice	0	✓	✓	0	✓	✓	
	Morning Chore	✓	✓	✓	0	✓	✓	
	Evening Chore	✓	✓	0	✓	✓	✓	
BARBARA	Room	✓	✓	✓	0	✓	✓	
	Music Practice	✓	✓	✓	0	✓	0	
	Morning Chore	0	✓	✓	✓	✓	0	
	Evening Chore	✓	✓	0	✓	✓	✓	

ture of school routine. A reward at the end of the chart is not always necessary; the immediate recognition and reinforcement after having completed the assignment can be enough. A chart that assigns jobs is very helpful, but a chart that also gives a place for a star or smiley-face carries a reward with it: "I've done something" or "I am finished." The child's self-esteem rises because she has a sense of control over the little tasks of her own life.

Ice-cream sundae chart. When you want your child to work toward a goal such as doing a better job on the dishes for a week, try an Ice-Cream Sundae Chart. The children build their sundaes step-by-step, earning another scoop of ice cream or topping with various accomplishments. Although they are

working toward a goal several days away, immediate reinforcement would come when the parent inspected the kitchen
and then let the children draw what they have earned on the
chart. They might choose to draw a dip of ice cream for each
of the first three days, then hot fudge, nuts, and whipped
cream.

Some people will argue that such tactics are nonsense—just
bribery. If you are a typical family, you will probably have a
treat of some kind during the week anyway. The treat could be
from the ice-cream shop or created at home. But if you could
get your children to see the pan left on the stove, the stickiness
on the counter, and the crumbs on the floor, and include them
with the kitchen clean-up for six days, your chances of a better
clean-up next week, even without the sundae incentive, are
much greater than before. We cannot promise the children will
not try to get you to offer another sundae next week, but now
that they know that you know they can do a better job in the

kitchen, you are standing on firm ground. Also, give verbal comments (social reinforcements) with the concrete reward of the sundae because these help to build an intrinsic reward system. Later the ice cream can be withdrawn, and the social reward and their feeling of accomplishment will be sufficient.

The treasure hunt. DeAnna created a treasure hunt for her six-year-old. She handed him the first note, which read, "Empty the trash." A note taped on the bottom of the trash basket said, "Shake the bathroom rugs." The third note (pinned to the bottom of the rug) told him to wash the legs on the kitchen chairs. Under one of them was a final envelope with a quarter in it and a note that stated, "You can buy a treat from the ice-cream man today." This game carried the mutual understanding that the assigned work would be done before collecting the reward.

Another variation would be to have the child finish all his assignments, and then go on a treasure hunt with clues to find the surprise. The Monson family has used a string winding through many parts of the house and yard to find a reward. This string could also be used with notes attached to assign jobs. It could be tied to the end of the broom to sweep the floor, wrapped around the furniture polish, or through a drawer with cleaning instructions. The end of the string could be in a suitcase or clothes dryer, with a little treat attached. The rule is that the string has to be wound up as they go and followed from beginning to end, doing jobs along the way.

Race car chart. The very young or immature child wants an immediate reward, but as children grow older, we can help them work for longer-range goals, perhaps using a progressive chart like the Race Car Chart. Set a goal such as taking out the trash every day for two weeks or even practicing music. Draw a pattern similar to the ones you see on game boards and pick a marker, in this case a race car. Each day, if the goal is reached, move the marker closer to the goal. It could be attached with a pin, tape, or magnet. Give generous recognition as the car moves along the track. If you find the child is not

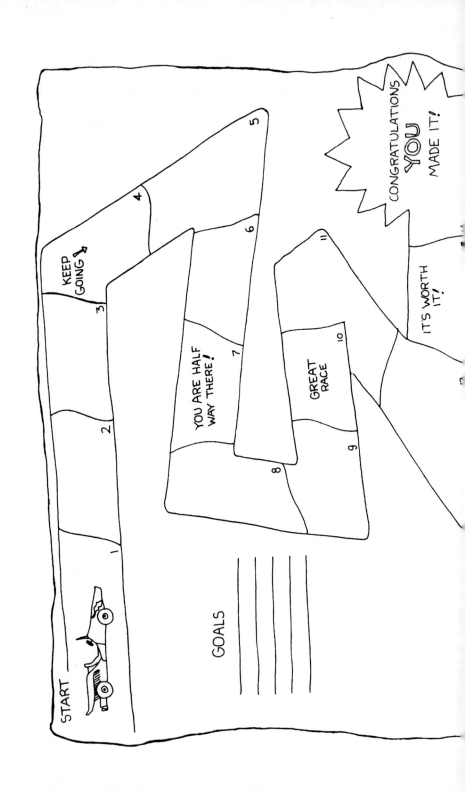

progressing, perhaps modification or re-evaluation is necessary. This chart could be created on the front of the refrigerator with colored tape, using magnets as markers.

Climb the ladder or bean stalk. Mary's son consistently dropped his coat in the living room and his books on the kitch-

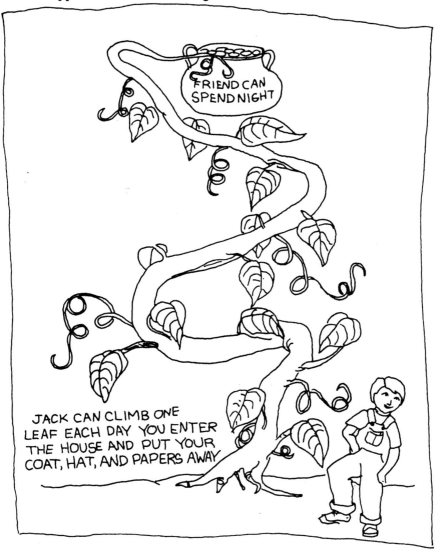

en table after school. She drew the Bean Stalk Chart to change the habit. Mary made sure there was a place to store his things and that he understood where they belonged. She drew the bean stalk (or it could be a ladder) on a large piece of poster board. A chart used for measuring height could also be purchased. A paper doll was used to progress toward the top as each milestone was reached. Choose a habit that needs improvement and measure progress as the figure moves, all the while reinforcing the positive behavior.

Marbles.　Try using game tokens as a progress reward system. "When you have earned twenty marbles, I will play Chinese checkers with you." It would probably have to be a game the child likes and one with a number of playing pieces. He would need to understand what tasks must be done to earn enough tokens to play the game. (Clean sink is worth two marbles, and so forth.) Collect earned marbles or other markers in a plastic bowl, where they can be seen and counted. Checkers, chess, Battleship, Scrabble, dominoes are just a few of the games that could be used. The reward is given in adult time—a commodity cherished by most children.

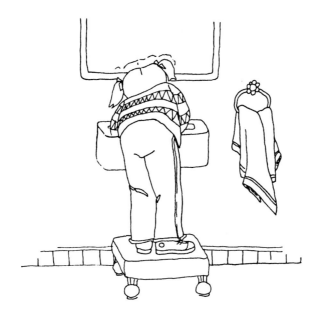

5: Teaching Them How to Work

If you want the children in your home to work, you will have to teach them. Sorry to say, they probably will not learn to work simply by example. You will have to show and tell, inspect and praise, and it isn't something that is accomplished in a day. But it can be tremendous fun to see a child's progress because it is so measurable. Children are usually capable of doing much more than is asked of them. We have a tendency to treat our own children as being two years younger than other adults treat them. There are breakdowns in getting kids to work, and many times it is because we have missed teaching a step in the job process. This is a chapter to be reread when having difficulty. How well children learn to work depends on five things. We will discuss the first four in this chapter.

LEARNING DEPENDS ON

1) The child's learning style
2) Work techniques
3) Teaching methods
4) Supervision
5) Incentives and consequences

LEARNING STYLES

Does your child work best alone or with others? Is she a reader or a listener? Is he influenced more by peers or by family? Each child learns differently, taking in messages from the world in a unique combination of ways. Research has helped educators identify numerous distinct learning preferences in people. They know that some students do well in traditional classrooms while others do best in open living areas with more freedom. At home you can also identify some of your child's preferred ways of gathering information by asking the following questions. Their answers will reveal whether their style is to do things alone, with others, or with family members; whether directions are clearer for them when heard rather than seen in print; and whether they like detailed step-by-step instruction rather than a freer atmosphere, where they discover the best way to do something with limited guidance.

"Would you rather work by yourself, with a friend, or with Mom or Dad?"
Style: Individual, Group, or Family

"Should we use a chart to show your responsibilities, or can
I just tell you what you should do?"
Style: Reader or Listener

"Do you want me to explain carefully how to wash the car
or would you rather read and follow the directions on the
can of car wash yourself?"
Style: Detailed Instruction or Discovery

Most children have several preferred styles; a strong identification with only one method is rare. Keep in mind that the
younger child tends to be more family oriented than the older
child. Some children may just like to work with others more
than alone, whether they be family members or peers. Consider the example of Erica, an eight-year-old, who spends every
free minute with her nose in a book. Her mother's words seem
to go in one ear and out the other. Erica's style is the written
word. A note that lists her job assignments will have more impact than will constantly telling her what must be done. In the
same family, John likes to talk, and to listen intently as his father reads to him. John can be told what needs to be done and
does it—he is a listener! Some children like to work with a
group of people. For them a "family clean-up hour" will pro-
duce more help than an assignment to work alone. Other children enjoy private time and do an excellent job working
independently.

The incentives and teaching techniques you use with your
children can be structured to fit their individual learning
styles. If Tom is influenced by friends more than family, use
incentives to encourage better work habits that reward with
privileges, like having a friend spend the night, or going to a
movie with several friends. The younger child can be motivated by the promise of playing a game with Mom or Dad after
work is finished.

Watch and listen to your children for clues of their particular learning preferences, fitting the job method to that style—it could make a difference in how easily they learn and how willingly they cooperate.

SHOW AND TELL STEP-BY-STEP

Let us suppose we are going to teach a five-year-old boy how to clean the bathroom. We need to be conscious of:

1. Breaking the job down into learnable parts
2. Teaching the proper method
3. The physical arrangement of the equipment and supplies

We won't give him responsibility for the whole room. Let's try three tasks: scouring the sink, polishing the chrome, and shaking the rug. In thinking of the supplies; is the cleanser where he can get it? What do you want him to use, a cloth or a sponge? (Hopefully not the face cloth.) Is it where he can get to it? Can he reach the sink? Maybe a step stool is needed. When it comes to teaching the proper method, you will give instructions about how much cleanser to use, and mention getting the scum around the drain and not putting the cleanser on the chrome handles. When he shakes the rug, teach him to roll it up and carefully carry it outside so that the bits of dirt don't fall off on the way. In the beginning, new training takes lots of show and tell. Go with the child every day as he cleans the bathroom, gradually decreasing your physical help but continuing the encouragement until he has mastered it at least *three times* by himself. Encouragement and positive comments need to be made often at this stage. "It does look better when that brown stuff around the drain is gone." "The handle shines so nicely, you can even see yourself in it." You are involving not only the child's physical senses in the job, but emotions as well. In this case, good emotions are shaping work attitudes: "It looks so nice, I can do it, and I like it better this way." When this child gets older, such time and detail aren't needed and you can rely more on verbal instructions. But remember, even as an adult, it is easier to cook crepes for the first time after you have seen someone else cook them. (Psychologists call this *modeling*.)

Break the job down into manageable parts. You can't just tell a child to go do the laundry without teaching him how. He has to know how to sort the clothes, operate the washer, select a proper drying procedure, fold, and so forth. Each of these categories can be divided into smaller parts. For the child, concepts are easier to remember than rote details. For example, when trying to teach sorting the soiled laundry, you might talk about dividing according to color, soil, and type of fabric, but also include association concepts like: "This skirt is made out of the same fabric as your jeans so we will put it in with the denims, but will we put it with Brother's jeans or Dad's greasy coveralls?" Teach them to analyze for themselves. It might help to post a chart in the laundry area as a quick reference for the correct procedure. Clarify instructions and watch out for double meanings.

Children aren't the only ones who get themselves into bigger messes than they can clean up. Has the kitchen ever been so littered that you didn't know where to start? Did you wish there was someone to help? Sometimes we have trouble knowing where to start because everything seems to have something else as a prerequisite—you can't start washing the dishes until there is a place to put the clean ones. Such an elephant needs to be divided into smaller parts so it can be accomplished. Put away the clean dishes that are in the drainer or dishwasher. Empty the sink. Fill it with hot soapy water. Put all the silverware in the sink and wash that much. Dry that much. Fill the sink with dishes again. Clean off a two-foot square on the counter, and so forth. Here again, a chart above the kitchen sink explaining these small steps may be helpful. Even as an adult, Bonnie finds she cannot force herself to deep clean the kitchen all at once. She takes one little section a day—one cupboard or the refrigerator today, the stove tomorrow. Although doing the whole job is not beyond her physical limitations, she can't cope with it mentally. But after a week of doing one section each day, she says to herself, "Why, I almost have this kitchen done. I bet I can finish it today." These are techniques for dividing work into small, manageable areas. Krista, a well-loved baby-sitter, gets the children to pick up toys and clothes by color grouping, a little bit of the Mary Poppins theory: "Let's pick up everything red."

We all hesitate to enter a tunnel when we can't see the end, for fear of not getting out. Weeding the garden could sound like a long tunnel, but dividing it up into four-foot-square sections with a rope or just requiring one row to be done a day isn't as overwhelming. Rather than saying "Let's pick up the house," declare a twenty-pick-up (each person picks up and puts away twenty items), or a five-minute pick-up, offering a foreseeable end. Keep in mind that, after the job is done, giving them another task squelches the incentive to get the first one finished. "Why hurry? If I get this row of beans weeded, Dad will just make me do another one." Telling them where the end is helps them look beyond this task to freedom.

Give notice of upcoming work periods, keeping them short and successful. At most elementary schools, a warning bell rings five minutes before the final bell, which signals the beginning of school. Advance warning of pending work helps secure cooperation. A standard routine such as morning chores before school or play or evening chores at five o'clock have built-in advance notice. This saves what the kids call unfair surprises. Other early warnings could be for extra work days: "Saturday we'll work in the yard until noon." Issuing a five- or ten-minute warning before dinner is ready or play time is over contributes to the general feeling of fairness in a family.

How can we motivate the procrastinator? Try a lead-in activity to start a project or to get in the mood. Ask, "What are you willing to do to this room?" Sometimes just working on it for fifteen minutes can get the child over the hang-up. Reinforcing it with a preferred activity often helps the child get into a project he is hesitant to do. Work before fun. Going to the library and swimming don't have the same appeal to all children. Take an inventory of what your child likes to do so you'll know natural interests, learning styles, and possible incentives. For the younger child, a typical preferred activity is a bedtime story. The parent might tell the child that when he is ready for bed, with pajamas on and teeth brushed, he will read the story. To get a little more mileage out of the incentive, the parent could set a timer and say, "If you are ready for bed in ten minutes, I will read a story." There is a point, however, when the incentive is overshadowed by an overwhelming job. It may be expecting too much to say, "When *everything* in your room is put away, I will read a story." Sometimes the technique of giving a negative reinforcement or mildly unpleasant punishment will work. "No TV until your clothes are put away" is a negative reinforcer. Give the child a choice and then provide an escape from the discipline when the child performs the task.

Consider the physical arrangement, equipment, and supplies—make it easy for them to succeed. Guests at the McCullough home have a hard time finding a cup for drinking because they are stored below the counter where the children can put them away when emptying the dishwasher or get them out to set the table, all without parental help. Make it as easy as possible for the child to do for himself. Is there a hook on which to hang his coat? Is his bed the kind he can make by himself? (Bunk beds and double beds are hard for children to make.) Also consider whether there are too many items in the area for the child's managing capabilities. Maybe a smaller broom would be better for sweeping.

Organize a maid basket in which to keep the basic cleaning supplies: glass cleaner, general cleaner, disinfectant, rags, and paper towels. Having the child take the maid basket with him to clean will encourage a more thorough job. *Caution: Keep unsafe supplies elsewhere.* Be sure to establish a safe storage location for such supplies, where smaller children cannot get to them. Don't be afraid to label shelves to show where things go. Trace the outline of the scissors or hammer with a felt-tip marker to show where it belongs. Write out instructions where helpful. Leave notes here and there: "Please rinse out the sink after brushing teeth." Look for ways to arrange the physical environment so the child can be successful.

It is interesting how clothes affect attitude, actions, and performance. Being fully dressed is part of having the right atmosphere for working. How people work reflects their feelings about themselves. Have the child get dressed, comb hair, and brush her teeth. Even the type of shoes can make a difference in work attitudes. House slippers hint that you are not fully there to work, but are unconsciously in the mood for lounging—and your work may be slower.

Sherolyn found color coding can be a way of making things easier for her child. A newspaper article told about a mother

of quintuplet girls who dressed each baby in the same color every day so she could tell them apart. At first, Sherolyn thought that was unfair; surely the girls would grow up to hate their colors. It was, however, a way to make the girls individuals, not just a group. Sherolyn adapted this idea to her children's possessions, but not necessarily to the color of their clothes. She assigned each of her three children a color; red, yellow, and blue because they are the primary colors and easy to remember. (Mom has green and Dad has purple.) Then she tagged their clothes in the back with a half-inch square of polyester fabric, sewing the swatches into some items of clothing and attaching them to others with gold safety pins. This makes it easy for any member of the family to fold and sort the laundry. Embroidery thread was used on the toes of socks. That way Mom's nice white tube socks didn't end up in her teenage son's pile. Sherolyn bought plastic cups in these colors for the mug rack in the bathroom, to make getting a drink easy and save filling the dishwasher with fifty glasses every day. She used the same colors when buying things like scrapbooks and toothbrushes. Permanent felt-tip pens were used to mark other things. (These could also be the colors used on the family activity calendar.) All of this helped the children to be individual, have their own, and keep it easy. One more thing. Sherolyn ordered two hundred labels from her local fabric store (about two cents each) that said Elrich Family, to sew in clothing. Before a new pair of gloves or new sweater can be worn the first time, the rule is that it has to have a label, making it easier to keep track of possessions. When the kids got navy-blue down coats, just like everyone else in the school, she sewed a little appliquéd figure on the outside to make them easily identifiable. She did the same thing with stocking caps. Even though the Elrich Family tag was on the inside, an appliquéd frog or flag was on the outside, for first-glance recognition.

Teach proper work methods so progress can be seen. Show the child how to work from the outside to the inside, taking care of the clutter scattered around the room before digging into the closet. Starting with the closet first only makes a double mess. Pick up the biggest things and then the smaller things. The bed is usually the biggest item in a bedroom. When it is cleaned off and made up, the room looks seventy-five percent better. Eric commented, "My room seems so much cleaner, and all I've done is made my bed." (An unmade bed is like a signal: "It's okay to leave everything out today.") Work in clockwise direction around the room or from the back of the room to the door so as not to work over an area already cleaned. Learn to pick up before the mess becomes monstrous. Stop life and make time after each play period and just before eating or going to bed to allow time to pick up. If you don't, how can you expect picking up to be a habit? At first it will take great effort, but it will become second nature.

There will be cleaning methods peculiar to your nature or the physical structure of your home that need to be taught. If the disposal isn't working, the garbage will be scraped into the wastebasket. Tell your children why you put the lettuce on the lower shelf of the refrigerator (so it won't freeze), and tell them to put a lid on the leftovers because the frost-free feature pulls all the moisture out of the food and because the food will pick up other flavors. We can't guarantee your children will follow all of your directions, but if they understand the principle, it is more likely to happen.

Insist on order. We subconsciously judge our homes by the impression we get as we come through the door. A custodian said, "When the restrooms and entrances of a building are clean, you assume the whole building is clean." We are not so worried about what visitors think as about how the family feels about themselves and their home. Filth is just plain unhealthy. Clutter causes confusion, and wastes time. But a sterile house is also uncomfortable. The goal might be for the home to be tidy most of the time. One man complained that the house was always messy—which it wasn't. The problem was that he entered the home through the garage and into the laundry room, which was piled high with clothes to be mended and folded, and that was his impression of the whole house.

It is important to insist that things not be dropped everywhere and anywhere in the house. In some homes, you can walk in and "read" everything that has happened: The dog won a ribbon for the curliest tail (the certificate is lying on the stereo), a new recipe book arrived (it is on the coffee table), school notices and bills have collected on the kitchen table, and so forth. Make a place for the mail and all the school notices until they can be dealt with. Maybe it will be an in-out file for the mail. The McCulloughs have a "pile-it" corner in the kitchen, (which cannot be easily seen), set aside for "temporary parking" of such items, but they don't allow every flat surface in the house to become a collecting spot. One mother, who started a campaign against the "drop-it" habit, put up a sign on the table as a reminder of the new emphasis. "No Parking. Violators will be charged 10¢ tow-away fee."

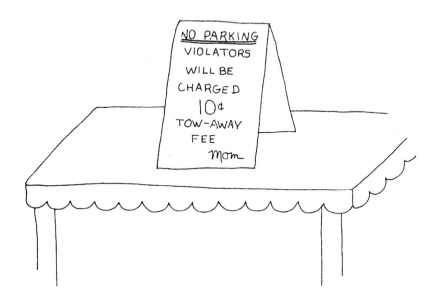

Many parents complain about children leaving a trail of coats and books behind them as they walk in the house. Create a place to put such items. Install hooks and shelves in a front closet. Then insist that the children use them. Even a box behind a chair for school books is better than books everywhere. Leaving things out in the main living areas gives an illusion of clutter that affects the family morale. A wise man said long ago, "By small and simple things are great things brought to pass." It may be the control and order of little things that makes a home run smoothly.

Make a time for work. Will your child work in the morning, after dinner, Saturday morning, or Friday afternoon? Having a set time every day or every week will help the child accept the assignment and plan other activities around home responsibilities. To improve cooperation, make this decision together in family council. Contrary to the pleadings of your children, efficiency will improve if friends are not allowed during work time. They will need time, without playmates, to work, and you will need to regulate that work. One mother set the rule that her children would not be available to play with neighborhood friends until noon, to give time for chores, music practice, and quiet play. Another mother preferred nine-to-twelve and three-to-five play periods. A third mother takes a more flexible approach, but says, "no play or TV until chores and bedroom are finished." Your decision should depend on the children's ages, interests, the weather, and your schedule. Perhaps you could set up a signal for play time, like the family with a swimming pool, who raised a red flag when it was "free swim."

HOME MODELS

Make the child believe this job is possible by giving him two types of models: a personal model and a standard for a good job. To offer a human model, be careful when using siblings or friends because resentment might spring up. It is better to use the child himself as a model by referring to past successes. "You did this . . . , you can probably do this. . . ." For example, when Eric Monson was struggling with his new paper route in Colorado, his mother pointed out how hard the route had been in Michigan, too, but that it was easier after he had memorized the route. Another time his mother gave encouragement by saying, "You wrote a nice story about Indians. I bet you can write a good one about President Lincoln." Then she did something about it by taking him to the library. Building on past successes serves as a model for the child, helping him believe it is possible. Mentioning only the good part and not the wrong, the extinction technique, also helps create his own success model because it emphasizes what the child is already doing well. Using the same patience and pleasant comments, pretend your child is the neighbor's child. It's interesting how nicely we treat "strangers" but are negative in the familiar atmosphere at home. A positive attitude moves toward something, and a negative attitude moves away from it. A child who is constantly neglecting, forgetting, or procrastinating her chores is moving away from the goals and needs more positive success at the job to serve as her model.

Try using examples and nonexamples. "Four times five equals twenty-one is a nonexample. Giving an example of how it doesn't work may make the children more aware of the correct process. Using a little furniture polish on the mirror and then comparing the results with the results of using window cleaner may make the point. Most of us at one time or another have confused salt with sugar—a nonexample.

Be sure to discuss improving the method rather than attacking the personality. Avoid bringing in all past mistakes by using such words as always, never, or every time. You could use yourself as a model. Instead of telling the child to put more soap in the dishwater, you could say, "Sometimes I have to add more hot water and soap to get all the grease off the dishes." The choice is still the child's. "I find it best to bring all the wastebaskets to the kitchen and empty them into the plastic garbage bag. In case the bag should break, it is easier to clean up." (This parent is using himself as model and offering "advice.") If the child chooses another method, fine. He is not defying a parental command, but if the garbage bag breaks on the carpet, guess who gets to clean it up?

A child models best when he has already had a little bit of experience because it puts him in a position to observe and evaluate. If he goes to a friend's house and helps them wash dishes, he just might observe the advantages and disadvantages of their techniques compared to those used in his own home. The child will begin picking up information from other homes as a baby-sitter or friend, from grandparents, businesses, and at school. A reserve of experiences will be stored on which he can build the satisfying feeling, "I have seen it done; I believe I can do it, too."

JOB STANDARD MODEL

The second type of model is a standard of acceptable work. How often has a child tried to tell her parent, "But you didn't tell me that was part of the job," switching the blame of an incomplete job to the parent. If the adult is very busy or the home has other children, the parent may not be sure if the child is right or not. Try writing a job description for each room or job in your home. When Bonnie did this, it only took about thirty minutes and it helped her decide, in detail, what needed to be done and how often. No matter who was working, whether it was the regular or substitute, they knew exactly what must be done. The job description saves misunderstandings with the children and can help them self-evaluate. It is a measure for parents to use, taking them out of the "bad-guy" spot, and giving the child the responsibility for checking on herself.

Following are the cleaning specifications for the McCullough home. They were typed on index cards and tacked in the closet or behind the curtains of the appropriate rooms. Make your written standard so explicit that a stranger could walk in and understand exactly what should be done.

GUIDED-DISCOVERY QUESTIONING

Guide a child into discovering for himself what still needs to be done by asking questions. "Standing here at the doorway, how does it look?" "Is there something you could do to the drawers to make them look better?" (Close them.) When offering help, leave the responsibility with the child by asking, "Would you like me to help?" But also give him the chance to discover what needs to be done: "What would you like me to do?" Children need to be taught to see disorder and dirt as the adult sees it. "Did you notice . . . ?" However, don't ask ques-

CLEANING SPECIFICATIONS
(to be tacked in closets):

Front Room
Daily:
Put away books and toys
Close piano; put bench under
Straighten cushions
Put newspapers neatly under
   table in far corner
Vacuum traffic areas

Weekly: (Saturday)
Vacuum carpet
Dust all furniture
Take newspapers to garage
Damp-wipe around door
Shake rugs
Sweep porch

Bathroom
Daily:
Pick up all hair equipment
   and straighten counter
Pick up toys and clothes
Straighten towels
Scour sink and polish
   chrome
Wipe off back of toilet
Shake rug

Weekly:
Scour toilet bowl
Wash towels
Wash brushes and combs
Polish mirrors
Sweep and mop floor

Bedrooms
Daily:
Make bed
Pick up clothes
Fold and put away pajamas
Keep top of bed and chest neat

Weekly:
Dust
Vacuum
Straighten drawers
Change bed sheets
Damp-wipe around door

Family Room
Daily
Pick up toys and books
Straighten blankets and pillows

Weekly:
Vacuum carpet
Wipe TV and around doors
Dust

Kitchen
Daily:
Rinse and put dishes in dishwasher
Refill cold drinking water
Cover leftovers and put in
   refrigerator
Wash pans and serving bowls
Dry pans and serving bowls
Shake rugs
Sweep floor
Scour and polish sink
Wipe off counters and table
Put away chairs
Fold down table

tions that build guilt or demand confessions: "Why is your room such a mess?" How often has a parent gone into a messy bedroom and told the child to put everything away and received the answer "It is put away; that's where I keep it." The inspection chart used by the Monsons (as shown on page 150) was a good method for helping their children know what Mom was checking. They were given a copy of the grading chart to inspect for themselves, after Sue had checked it, and they saw their bedrooms in a new way.

One father plays a game with his kids which is patterned after the observation game. The observer gets a minute to look at twenty items on a tray before it is taken away, and then tries to list them all. This father challenges his young children to put away twenty things, and then Dad tries to remember as many of them as he can. This trains the child to notice what is out of place. After a while the child may put away little tiny things to trick Dad, but that's okay because awareness is developed. It is a way of giving immediate, positive social attention to what has been put away, rather than negative reminders about the items left out. Dad's attention is such a premium, the kids love it.

As adults, once we have become good at a job, it is hard to realize there could be another way to do it. An optimistic young adult, Joan, went to Israel to live in a communal kibbutz. Even though all the work positions were treated with dignity, Joan said, the individualism was gone. When someone was assigned to clean the dining room floor, there were supervising experts who had been streamlining the job for forty years. They were so efficient that a drain had been installed in the center of the dining room floor. The floor could be hosed down and wiped with a squeegee such as we use on windows. They knew which side of the room to start on and which way to make the strokes. They were so efficient, there was no room for individual interpretation or personal discovery. One woman carries negative memories of her mother picking at her for every little thing, even yelling at her for sweeping dirt away from her with the broom rather than toward her. The daughter preferred the "away" strokes because it kept her shoes from getting dusty. In your home, you have a right to expect a minimum standard, but not to dictate every action. Self-discovery can be a great motivator. "Tell me how you think this would be best done?" It could be taken so far as to ask the child to write down what she thinks would be the best method for cleaning the bathroom, and share them with the family. Parents get in a habit of issuing commands, especially when we are very busy, and forget to let the child do the discovering. To discover an answer or method is better than to be told. The discovered answer is remembered longer because it involves an analytical process in the mind rather than using just the ears. Most questions automatically arouse curiosity. Use them often.

Finger plays for chores. Teach young children to take on their own responsibilities with a simple reminder system on their fingers. Instead of demanding "Is your bed made?" the

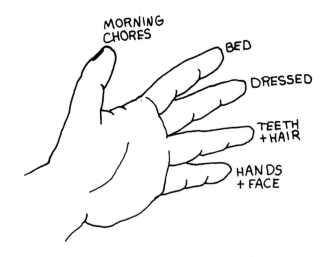

parent can ask "What do you have left to do this morning?" and the child can answer "I still have to make my bed and brush my teeth." You have put the responsibility where it belongs. What makes this work? The parent teaches the child a sequence of key words or phrases, one for each finger. Each day, the child runs through the list on his fingers and does each task. When he is finished, he is ready to go to school or play.

To begin this in your home, list the tasks that need to be done every day. Pick a noun as the key word to represent each job. Arrange them in sequential order. Brushing teeth and washing would come before dressing, to prevent splashes on clean clothes. The sequence the McCullough family uses is as follows: (1) hands and face, (2) teeth and hair, (3) dressed (including shoes and socks), (4) bed (including room pick-up), (5) morning chore, or just toys for the youngest children. They don't include eating breakfast on the list because they don't have a problem in that area. Use the same set of words for all children in a family. Added responsibility can be attached to the symbol word as the child matures, but don't try to change the key words. For instance, under the third category, bed, a four-year-old may not be asked to vacuum his bedroom, but by the time he is seven, vacuuming might be part of his responsibility.

When the child needs a reminder, the parent says, "What have you finished so far?" After going over the sequence of words on his fingers, the child will answer, "Well, I've swept the stairs and made my bed, but I still have to brush my teeth." She has been the one to recognize what must be done, and she is on the way to self-rule. This memory device of learning the morning routine on fingers can be started as young as two years or as late as seven years, and will last a lifetime. The most important point is that the child learns to answer the questions "Am I finished yet?" and "What must I still do?"

The McCulloughs started teaching their youngest child personal responsibility at two and a half years. After dressing him, Bonnie takes his hand in hers and points to one finger at a time (like playing piggy-wiggy). "Now, Mattie, let's see what you have to do. Hands and face?" (He nods yes whether he has done it or not.) "Teeth and hair? No? Let's do that now." When he has finished brushing, she begins again. "Dressed? Yes, and your shoes are on too! Good! Bed?" (Nods yes.) "No, I'll help you. Toys? We'll pick up your books after we have made the bed." Taking him by the hand, she leads him patiently through each activity. Naturally, he was too young in the beginning to make his bed, but he stood next to her while she did it. In a year or so, he was climbing up at the head of the bed and Bonnie was tossing the quilts to him. Then he would put the pillow on and cover it up. When they were all finished, Bonnie gave a positive comment and then told him he could play because all his chores were finished. He left feeling grown up and successful. A bonus: Mom had fewer interruptions because all of his immediate needs had been taken care of first.

After the basic hygiene and chores are taken care of, a child is free from parental promptings. He feels rewarded for his accomplishment because he is ready for whatever opportunity comes up. He can go for a ride to the store or play with a friend. Once the basic responsibilities are established, parents can be more than just reminders. They can be leaders instead of herders.

SUPERVISION

If you want to achieve the goal of getting your child to work at home, be available to supervise—not as a taskmaster with a whip but as a coach, to direct, help, encourage, and motivate. It won't happen if the parent is off in the basement ironing or doing a complicated job while the children (four to ten years) are supposed to be working. On a construction job, organized under a labor union, a supervisor cannot participate in the actual labor. This policy does not apply at home. A little friendly help from the parent now and then fosters a "caring" attitude in the home. Being reachable lets the child know that if he needs assistance, it is available.

When the parent is near the action, expressions of encouragement on how well the job is coming and appreciation when the job is completed are more likely to be given—helping to fill the basic human need for self-esteem. When these verbal rewards are given, the child is more likely to work again for you. The child also wants to know, "Did I do it right?" One neighbor commented that even as a teen she never worked when her mom was gone, even though the hours dragged and there was nothing else to do. She needed adult feedback. Unconsciously, some children feel that even negative chastisement is better than nothing at all. Kids like a little reminding as a signal their parents care. As children get older, they work alone for longer periods of time. There are even a few teens who prefer to get their work done before their parents get home. Part of this is a feeling of grown-up-ness. You will find the logic quite interesting. Teens say they do their chores before their parents get home:

Because it's easier and I can do them my way

Because we don't have to do a good job

Because my mom won't do things that I want if I don't do my chores

Because I really love them and don't believe in cheating on work

To surprise them when they get home

Because I don't like a dirty house

Make sure the child has enough practice at succeeding with a job. The more we do something, the easier it becomes. The first time you make a new recipe, it takes almost twice as long as the second time. There are children who prefer a chore as-

signment for a week or two because they become efficient at
the job.

Should I call a child back to re-do a job? Yes, if there has
been a specific rule infraction or the child has tried to slip by
with a half-way job. But remember this: If you are always calling your child from play or interrupting an activity, you may
one day wonder why your child doesn't stick to one project for
more than a few minutes. One mother found it worked, especially in the summer, to keep a list of things that needed attention and brought it forth at the next work time, giving the
children some "free time" between the work sessions.

For some jobs, we not only need the skill, but we have to
develop the self-motivation to do it every day—for example,
bed making. It not only takes help to learn the skill, it takes
parental help, especially supervision, to learn the mature work
habit of following through—a principle not usually considered. We assume that because the child has the skill, *he can do
it.* The reason he often can't, is because he doesn't have the
habit yet. Establishing the habit takes much longer than teaching the skill. Parents can help establish firm habits by offering
proper supervision, providing practice, exercising patience,
and yes, by dangling carrots—incentives. Proper supervision
takes "super vision."

While you are working together, take time to talk, but don't
lecture. Talk about future plans, what happened at school, an
exciting book, anything. This can be a time of communication.
Thirty years ago, children spent most of their lives in close,
side-by-side working associations with their parents and relatives. This togetherness helped the child model, pick up similar values, and learn to work. In our society today, a child
spends less than fourteen minutes a week talking with his parents, which hardly represents competition for television,
school, and peers. Take time to talk *with,* not just talk *at,* your
child. If you run out of things to talk about, try telling jokes or
singing together.

6: Giving Positive Feedback

Why so much emphasis on the positive? Don't children need to be told when they are wrong or if the job doesn't pass minimum standards? Studies have proven that pointing out what's wrong doesn't bring about a change or even move as quickly toward the desired goal as does giving positive comments about acceptable or correct aspects of the job. A negative comment reinforces the wrong performance. A positive comment builds confidence and the desire to do better, to reap even more approval. We want our children to succeed, and we try so hard to help them—but often in the wrong way. Wayne's story is a classic example. He was nine years old and repeating the third grade. His art work was excellent, math skills were average, reading was at first grade level, English poor, self-concept very low, and in a social situation he withdrew, becoming a loner. His parents were well educated and provided him many opportunities. Wayne had undergone batteries of tests, all of which showed no apparent learning disability. What had gone wrong? The clue came at the first open house when his parents visited the classroom. The students had drawn pictures of their own houses and pinned them around a town map. The teacher was standing next to Wayne's mother, to hear her first comment as she studied the display. "Look how crooked this line is on Wayne's house!" his mother complained. "His perspective should be better." When the teacher pointed out that Wayne's house showed much more detail and perspective than any of the others, his mother was surprised. She had not noticed! Even Wayne's best area of achievement, his art work, was under the severe scrutiny of a parent's critical eye. Wayne had concerned, loving parents but their methods for getting him to achieve were negative rather than positive.

Statistics reported by Dr. Stephen Glenn of the Family Development Institute show that in the average home a child receives only one positive response for every twenty-one negative responses. (The dog even fares better.) In school, the ratio is thirteen negative to one positive. What are we doing to our children? Consideration of the following principles may help us be more positive with our children.

Evaluation should be positively pleasant. Wayne's parents forgot this important principle. One of the overriding purposes of parenthood is to build the child's positive self-concept. Good feedback from the parent nurtures this self-concept. The parents are two of the most significant people in the child's life. The negative, positive, conditional, or unconditional approval given by the parents can determine how successful the child can be at mastering a certain task.

Evaluation should be immediate. Do you remember studying many hours for a test and anxiously wondering about your score but not finding out the results until several weeks later? Or how about the job interview after which you have to wait for the promised call. In the book *Coping with Children's Misbehavior*, Rudolph Dreikurs says, "Children prefer being beaten to being ignored." The child strives for recognition, and the sooner it is given, the better. The time spent by parents giving feedback shows the child that his efforts are recognized.

What would your child do if he or she were asked, "Write one thing your parent told you that made you feel really good about yourself"? Would he sit and just look at the blank piece of paper, or would she write without hesitation? A person likes himself if he has been treated as if he is likable. Before saying something, stop and ask these questions: "Will what I say make this child feel good or bad about herself? Will it make her try harder or stop trying?" This is not always easy, because we have to like ourselves in order to respond so gallantly.

Give recognition for even the meagerest of accomplishments as your children learn new skills or practice old ones. We are not suggesting that you follow the child all day and comment on every little thing that is done. But appreciation and recognition can be tossed forth here and there, when you think of it. The positive has such great motivating power. There are situations where the parent is hard put to offer any positive feedback, where the outcome of work does not seem greater than zero, but there has to be something good that can be said. Praise and encouragement should be honest and specific or it can be seen by the child as phony or worthless. To tell John that his cake was the "best in the world" when it was flat only makes John feel defeated and distrust your word. But you could say, "It was so nice of you to take the time to bake this cake for us." In this case, the attention was focused on the effort made, not the end result.

At this point, it might be good to make a distinction between the words "praise" and "encouragement." Praise is usually offered after the job is completed. Praise words such as "good job" give approval at the end of a task. Try to keep these verbal rewards very specific. Encouragement is offered as fuel to keep going. Encouraging words such as "keep your chin up, you're almost finished" inspire children with hope, making them believe that the power behind them is greater than the problem before them.

Use the principle of shaping or reinforcing behavior that is *close to* the desired behavior. If you want your child to make her bed every day, but she only makes it four days a week, don't cause discouragement by scolding for the three days it wasn't made. Instead, give positive reinforcement for the measure of accomplishment she did achieve. Suppose a young boy picks up five books but leaves three on the floor. Commenting on the five he picked up is better than nagging about the other three. Shaping is the process of building toward that final goal of picking up all eight books.

Let the child judge her own work. Sue Monson had a very self-motivated fourth grade student one year, a child who enjoyed learning for the sake of knowledge and not for the token grade. At parent conference she asked the father, who happened to be a psychologist, how this intrinsic-reward system was developed. The father replied, "When Phil would bring home one of those awful papers from nursery school with paint splattered all over it and finger smudges, we would ask how he liked what he had made. Phil would look closely at his paper and say either he did like it or he thought it was a mess. He learned to judge his accomplishment instead of letting us always be the evaluators." A simple yet effective technique.

Focus attention on the learning experience, not just on the finished product. Trial and error is still a powerful teacher. Questions such as "How would you do this another time?" or "What did you learn from this experience today?" help the child evaluate, plan for the next time, and add credits instead of debits to the self-esteem account. Sharing an example from your own trial-and-error learning helps relax the atmosphere, bring a laugh, and open up communication. Recall such memories as the time Dad used milk powder instead of flour in the cookies. Generally your child wants to please you. Get full mileage from training by understanding and commenting on the growth that took place and sometimes ignoring the finished product.

Watch the labels you give your child. What do your children hear you say about them when you are talking on the telephone? Bonnie's husband gently pointed out that her description of their two-year-old, "destroying angel," was a negative label. What title is your child wearing on his T-shirt? Children tend to become what others tell them they are.

Stop and concentrate, or even count, to be sure you are giving positive strokes. Keep in mind that words of approval and encouragement are more important than any token incentive or punishment that can be given—and they are free, too. One older woman, whose children were all grown, commented, "I don't believe in all that positive-reward stuff. Kids should work because they are supposed to and if they don't, then punish them!" Yes, the punishment may stop an undesirable behavior, but it will not create the new, better habit as positive reinforcement will. Stop and think; would you enjoy working for a boss who never told you he appreciated your effort or that you were doing a good job? No. You would get away from that situation if you possibly could. It is the same for children, who are learning to work under the adult, or "parent-boss." They need encouragement. Picture the difference in a child's reaction as you hand her a set of cut out paper dolls on which is written several positive compliments or the same girl who has just been told four things wrong with her bedroom.

In our society, it is so easy to give negative rewards that the effort to do otherwise requires a constant conscious effort. Kaoru Yamamoto, in the book *The Child and His Image*, advocates a reward (praise)-to-punishment (negative feedback) ratio. "By reward [he means] anything that makes the child feel good about himself and his potential ability to master his environment ... [including] such behaviors as a pat on the shoulder, a warm smile ... or a simple 'Thanks.' By punishment [he means] anything that diminishes the child's sense of feeling like a worthwhile person. A frown, stony silence, deprivation of privileges, or a remark such as 'What's wrong with you again?' " Yamamoto finds that if the ratio of punishment to reward is four rewards to one punishment it will "help guide and direct a child's behavior."

Change your responses. Even though the goal is to change the child, in many cases it is best done by changing the parents' behavior; in this case positive rather than negative feedback. One mother set her goal to change the ratio of positive and negative responses. As incentive, she offered herself five dollars a day toward the new lamp she wanted. (Much cheaper than a psychologist.) To keep score, she bought a golf-stroke counter to wear on her wrist (a grocery tabulator could be slipped in a pocket, too). The first day, the results were fantastic. The behavior change in the kids was so delightful, the lamp hardly mattered. She continued to use the counter for several weeks to be sure her positive responses became a habit. This solution sounds so simple that many people refuse to try it.

Remember, parents who read and try new ideas will have "parent growing pains." They will notice things that are wrong that they haven't paid any attention to before. They might feel guilt for past actions or wish they had known this or that before. Whatever has happened in the past is gone. You did the best with the tools and knowledge you had. In a few years, these ideas may be outdated by new and even better methods. Guilt should lie not in mistakes, but in not trying and in not looking for better methods. Pick up from where you are and move forward with positive steps.

Use the list of 129 positive statements that follow to initiate creative responses. Your youngsters will enjoy hearing more than the traditional "good," "nice job," and "fine." Even the younger child likes hearing a big word like "stupendous," if you explain that it means great and wonderful. The child's self-concept soars and he may apply himself with triple effort to the task at hand. Brainstorm some other fun responses if these don't fit your nature. Tap your own imagination and use fun names from television shows such as *Wonderwoman* or *Superman,* pick from nursery rhymes or sports personalities, use whatever words make your child feel good. Try positive feedback. It works!

POSITIVE STATEMENTS THAT ENCOURAGE

What a worker!

An elegant job!

Clever worker!

Fantastic effort!

Keep your chin up!

I like the way you're working!

That looks like it's going to be a great job!

This kind of work pleases us very much!

I appreciate your helpfulness!

Now you've got the hang of it!

This is much better!

Keep up the good work!

You are learning so much!

What an efficient worker!

It's nice to work with you when you have such a happy attitude!

You work like a trooper!

Wow, you really stick to your job!

Excellent effort!

You catch on real fast!

Your independence is growing!

You have been a self-starter. Great!
You're doing much better!
You've just about got it!
Great improvement!
You're getting better————every day!
You're on the right track!
You must have been practicing!
Way to go!

POSITIVE STATEMENTS THAT COMPLIMENT OR PRAISE

Tremendous!
Mr. Clean approved!
Spotless work!
Wonderful!
Great!
You deserve a gold medal!
Hey, take a bow!
Applause is due!
Superior!
What skillful work!
A fine, fine job!
Swell, just swell!
Dandy!
Peachy!
An elegant job!
You've got it!
You did the topping on the cake!

This is above par!

You are a champ!

The best ever!

This room is fit for a king!

This room is fit for a queen!

It passed, excellently!

You should be proud of this!

This benefits us all!

What superbness!

Not bad, not bad at all!

Magnificent job!

Marvelous accomplishment!

Super!

This is a first-rate achievement!

Glorious work!

Superior!

This is choice!

Very nice————!

Fine work!

Grand!

This is dazzling work!

A-Okay!

You are a winner!

Thank you very much!

Much better!

This tops the best!

Hey, this is a bit of all right!

This is the best ever!

What a champion performance!

This is so neat, it's a knockout!

Your helpfulness has been superb!

Right on!

Your contribution adds beauty!

Nice!

Splendid!

Excellent!

Stupendous!

Wow!

Fantastic!

Super job!

Unbelievable!

First rate!

You get an A!

Way to go!

Out of this world!

As good as can be!

Aren't you proud of the way you worked today?

You must be pleased with your job!

That kind of job makes me happy!

Isn't it nice to have the work done!

You have done this very well!

Swell job!

You make me want to boast!

How proud I am of the way you did————!

This is in great shape!

What a bang-up job!

This is high-class work!

You deserve a star!

Wow, a golden worker!

This is worthy of praise!

You are a first-rate achiever today!

This job is one in a million!

This is top notch!

Prize work, for sure!

This is the tops!

This room is ready for display in a magazine!

This work is in a class by itself!

A-1!

Hurray, this is up to snuff!

You outdid yourself!

Beautiful!

You surpassed all expectations!

Wow, you certainly used your time wisely!

You must feel very capable!

Super! You kept your mind on your work!

Your work habits have greatly improved. You must be proud!

You made great use of your skills!

What a stupendous independent worker!

Your fine work has been noticed!

You gave this room the final touch of class!

You don't need much supervision now!

You should be proud of how consistently you've done your
work this week!

Your room reflects hard work!

Your cooperation is fantastic!

It's a pleasure to go into your neat room!

Wow, you have been so conscientious!

7: Offering Incentives and Rewards

Why are incentives, rewards, and logical consequences useful? Because they:

- Prove to the child that she can do it
- Motivate with outside forces until the inner motivation is developed
- Keep the task interesting
- Get the child over a fear
- Help him finish and feel successful

If a child is going to hurt himself, someone, or something, he has to be stopped by whatever means pops into your mind. But, if the problem is not so immediate, there is time to try other ways to change a bad habit or start a good habit. This is where incentives, rewards, and consequences can be used. It takes time to learn to use these devices, just as it takes time to learn to use a new appliance such as a microwave oven. Some parents find it stimulating to read at least one parenting book a year to get new ideas on how to use these and other principles.

Incentives and rewards are motivators from outside the child and can be anything the child likes: books, privileges, strokes, food, or money. A good incentive may be needed in the beginning of training or to perk up interest, but it can gradually be eliminated. They start to become bribes, however, when the reward has to keep getting bigger to initiate the desired behavior. We need to emphasize that incentives are not used all the time for everything. On the other side of motivation, consequences occur when the child makes a wrong choice. Natural consequences happen because of the nature of the world—if you don't wear gloves on your hands in freezing weather, they get cold. A logical consequence is structured by the adult to be the logical result of misjudgment on the part of the child. It usually involves withdrawing the related privilege or restoring the undone as much as possible. Consequences are not to be confused with threats. In fact, every action doesn't have a consequence. In the real world, for example, most of the time we don't get caught for speeding.

Incentives or reinforcers can be used as a reward when trying to change a behavior, when trying something new, or when the situation is slightly threatening. If you make a promise for a reward, you must keep it to maintain trust, but promises don't have to be made for everything. In the book *How to Teach Children Responsibility,* Harris Clemes and Reynold Bean state "Working for rewards is a way children develop a goal-orientation. . . . Concrete rewards help children establish concrete goals. . . . There are times in the child's life when material rewards seem to be most important. As children learn that material rewards can be gained by them as a result of their performance, their self-confidence increases, and their sense of responsibility grows. This allows them to develop alternative reward systems."

According to psychologist Marcia McBeath, there are three types of incentives: intrinsic, social, and extrinsic. The intrinsic reward is the good feeling the child gets when something has been done well. When someone gardens, sews, cooks or reads because he likes to or because he knows he'll feel good when he finishes, he is reacting to an intrinsic incentive. The extrinsic reinforcer—the grade, a movie, treat, or privilege—motivates from outside the person. These motivators can serve to entice the child to do something until she has the inner desire. The social reward is usually a verbal comment expressing appreciation, encouragement or awareness of a job well done. When the extrinsic token is combined with a social expression, the token can later be withdrawn and the social reinforcer will be sufficient.

Rewards and consequences are stimuli from outside to be used while the child develops the mature, intrinsic motivation and self-discipline from within. In this chapter, we deal mostly with positive motivators.

Incentives and rewards are fun because they can be planned with all the pleasure of anticipation or they can be spontaneous with the merriment of surprise, whereas consequences have to be logical, fair, and consistent. The following is a collection of rewards and incentives that we have tried or that have drawn our attention. You have to keep working to find the right blend of rewards and incentives to keep your child motivated. It is as though each child has his own secret combination and we have to find the right set of numbers to unlock them. Use the ideas that fit your mood and circumstance. If you have other ideas, we would love to hear them too.

VERBAL STROKES

As already discussed, social rewards are the most successful in bringing about change in a child's behavior. These verbal expressions of encouragement and appreciation don't cost money, either. Children change their behavior to receive these rewards or "strokes." Strokes can be positive or negative, and children prefer one over the other by the time they are seven or eight years of age depending on which satisfies their need for attention. Negative responses don't bring about positive behavior; they only reinforce the undesirable. If you want to encourage a behavior, then give positive comments about what is really right.

Strokes can be general: "You are a good girl." Strokes can be specific: "You did a nice job washing the car." (When you are complimenting a job, it is better to compliment the job well done than the personality.) Strokes come in varying degrees of vigor: "I'm proud of you!" or *"I'm really proud of you!"* More emphasis means the reward is greater. Positive strokes are the best rewards. We all seek them, we save them up, and they are building blocks of self-confidence. Serve them generously.

General strokes are often difficult to accept. "You are a good boy!" is too general because nobody is totally good. If the child can't honestly accept the compliment, he may be forced to do something to prove you wrong. For example, a baby boy had recently been born to the Gundersons. During a friendly visit from an old roommate, Anne Gunderson praised her three-year-old son with "Scott is such a good big brother!" After Anne told her friend good-bye, she discovered Scott in his brother's room vigorously "powdering" the baby. Powder dust filled the air and the baby was choking frantically. Scott had justified that he was not a "good big brother." Indeed, he resented the extra time and attention spent on the baby. Anne could have said, "Scott brings me diapers to help!" This specific comment would alleviate the need to retaliate by proving one wasn't so "good."

By making your positive strokes deal with specific details, the child knows what she or he did right. "I can tell by how smooth the covers are that you worked especially hard making your bed this morning!" or "I was so pleased to see you put your plate in the dishwasher without being asked." When complimenting the individual, keep in mind that a stroke that mentions a physical trait or something a child really isn't responsible for, such as "Becky, your hair is such a lovely color of red," isn't nearly so meaningful as a compliment directed toward her ability or personality: "Becky, you take such good care of your hair!" (ability) or "It's fun to be with you!" (personality). Positive reinforcement, encouragement, compliments, strokes, and appreciation will do a great deal in helping your child learn to do household chores or take care of personal grooming. If it is not your nature to give these verbal expressions, you may need to create some sort of tally system or incentive to help *you* change. By taking the time to make this change in your life to a positive response system, you will get *big* payoffs.

There are times, especially with the young child, when the parent needs to use a little forceful action to start the correct behavior. For example, Sylvia was trying to get her three-year-old to pick up the books spread all over the floor. She grasped the girl by the hand, took her to the books, put her left arm around her daughter's waist, and bending over together, they picked up and put away a book. Even though the action has been completely controlled, the mother could then offer verbal encouragement. "It looks better already. Now let's do another one." Soon, Sylvia could withdraw physically, but still help the child side by side. Sylvia had to insist on the first success in order to have something to build her positive comments on. As the child did more on her own, she had more successes to build upon. Success breeds success.

LOVE NOTES

Love notes can be a lot of fun once you start looking for ways to write your appreciation (social reinforcers). One morning, when Bonnie was tempted to scold five-year-old Mattie for dawdling, she decided to make his bed for him and put a smiley-face note on it that read, "A secret fairy was here and made your bed. Surprise!" He was thrilled and asked his mother to read it for him. He showed everyone the yellow circle and asked each if they had made his bed. He put the smiling face on his clothes line (a string from corner to corner of one wall on which school papers and art work were hung with clothes pins) and talked for days about the fairy making his bed. Sometimes such a charitable act will trigger other acts of kindness. Anyway, it was more fun than the usual scolding. Now, once in a while, when Bonnie and her husband Bob go to bed, they find a love note on the pillow: "I love you Mom and Dad."

At the elementary school, the children get "Happy Grams" and "Glad Grams" which are displayed on a large bulletin

board in the main lobby of school, the Hall of Fame. One says, "Shawna, sensational, you've passed the rhyming phrases test!" and she gets to take it home on Friday to show her parents—a good way to reinforce effort and achievement. One family has a wall in the den on which to put the "Happy Grams." They hung a big sign that read, "Warm Fuzzies, we all need them." Then they started putting up warm, fuzzy notes for each other. "Teri, thanks for helping today," or "October 9, the day Mom got the mending caught up."

The Johnson family started Good Deed Sheets for each child and parent to record for themselves the extra things they did for the family. This way, the family members didn't have to wait for someone else to notice their efforts. We all need to recognize the things we *are* doing—to have a sort of "victory list." Adding up accomplishments or good deeds can help build self-esteem.

GOOD DEED SHEET

I did these extra things to help. I know it takes just one person to make the world a better place. I want to be a helpful family member.

signed _____

Date _____   _Good Deed_ _____

_____   _____

_____   _____

_____   _____

_____   _____

RIBBONS, CERTIFICATES, AND COUPONS

Pam used the incentive method to motivate a habit change: taking off clothes right side out (saves lots of time on laundry day). Instead of nagging, she packed a suitcase with Dad's big pajama bottoms, socks, and sweat shirt. At family council, the game was to put on Dad's clothes and take them off *right side out.* That means pulling the pant leg and the sock from the toe instead of peeling them down from the top. Each child who was successful (and she made sure they all were) received a coupon redeemable for a treat. Then Pam explained that another coupon could be earned by each person whose clothes came through the laundry on wash day all right side out. After issuing success coupons for only three weeks, Pam had modified an undressing habit that had amounted to many work hours for her.

A year later, as a reminder (they had slipped a little), she handed out a blue ribbon with a gold seal on the top which read "Congratulations—Clothes Right Side Out." She awarded the ribbon to Jill at family council so everyone would see it—a method of ignoring the lack of effort by the other family members. Often, rewarding success of one motivates the others to the same action. Again, be careful not to foster the wrong kind of competition between siblings. The best kind of reward is when everyone has a chance to win: "Everyone who has clothes all right side out next week gets a blue ribbon."

Everyone loves to receive certificates. Make your own by using ideas from children's coloring books or newspaper ads. These could be awarded at family council, at dinner, or left propped against the bed pillow.

INSPECTIONS

At Glennon Heights Elementary School, the class with the cleanest room hosts a "mop doll" for a week. The custodian

gets to be the judge. There are a lot of tricks you can use to keep things interesting at home, too. On page 149 we described the point-inspection system for the bedroom. Pam Brace and Peggy Jones, two sisters living in Vancouver, Washington, trade off being house fairies to each other's families. One will dress in a ballerina costume, using a vacuum attachment for a wand, and show up at her sister's house for a bedroom check. Each person who passes the inspection gets a little wrapped gift (inexpensive trinket or game). If they don't pass, they do not get the gift—a logical consequence—but the incentive is strong to keep it neat for the next time. Little notes and tiny surprises are left by the house fairy from time to time. Two neighbors who heard about this idea, agreed to trade off inspections. They had regular, planned inspections every Saturday for three weeks and in between times the child's own mother left notes. When it was close to Easter, they were left in plastic Easter eggs. One such note read as follows:

> On my way to the Fairy's Track Meet
> I stopped in your room to take a peek.
> Your room was so nice, picked up and clean,
> I had to leave all twenty jelly beans.
>
> The House Fairy

For the child whose room wasn't neat, the note read as follows:

> On my way to the Fairy's Track Meet
> I stopped in your room to take a peek.
> Twenty jelly-bean-eggs were for you,
> But I had to subtract a few.
> Better luck next time!
>
> The House Fairy

PRIVILEGES

Work before fun gives incentive to get it done. Generally, a basic routine that must be done before school, television, or play is fair. The simple idea of having the child dress before breakfast helps him to do it in half the time it would take to dress after breakfast. An immediate incentive: "At one o'clock, everyone in the family whose room is cleaned and vacuumed can go with us for a family swim." When the time arrives, only those who have completed the task get the reward, even if it means hiring a baby-sitter. Be firm.

For the young child, immediate incentives are best, such as the daily star work chart shown on page 62. In the finger plays of morning routine (page 86), finishing is the immediate reward. The privilege is freedom after the responsibility has been met. The advantage of good supervision is that verbal expressions can also be dealt immediately. Put something less desirable before something more desirable. ("When you have your pajamas on, we will read a story." After you have finished your bedroom, we will go to the library.") That means you have to know what motivates your child—not everyone likes a story or the library.

Anything the child wants to do can be an incentive, but remember, not every privilege should hang on a mountain of work, because the motivation can be squelched. There are parents who use the next pending event to bleed the turnip. Keep the incentive simple and reasonable. The objective in the beginning is to help this child succeed and in the end, success is the greatest motivator.

FOOD

Food can be used as an immediate reward, especially to change behavior. For years we have heard how food brings about success with slow and retarded children. Special learning classes offer points to earn goodies for good work. Immediate food rewards can also be a tool to improve behavior and form good habits in normal children. Important principles for using this behavior modification are as follows: (1) work with only one behavior change at a time, (2) keep the task simple, (3) make the reward minimal, (4) be unwaveringly consistent in giving the reward only when all the desired behavior is performed.

Do you realize what five little M & M candies can do? They can motivate a child to sleep in his own bed, overcome the fear of going to Sunday school class alone, or get him to flush the toilet and wash his hands. They act as incentives and immediate rewards. Creating proper incentives is challenging, but it results in positive changes when coupled with positive strokes.

How do the M & M candies work? "I have five M & M candies in my pocket for you after Sunday School if you stay in your class." If the child doesn't quite make it, say, "I'm sorry, son. Perhaps next week you can stay with your teacher." Don't give the reward unless the behavior was completed. You may need to use a gentle one-time reminder of the pending reward beforehand: "I hope you sleep in your own bed all night, so you can have five chocolate-coated raisins in the morning." (Repeating the incentive over and over turns it into a bribe.) In the morning, praise and approval come with the candy reward: "I'm so proud of you for sleeping in your bed. I knew you could do it. Doesn't it make you feel good?" Remember that using the social or verbal recognition will make it easier to eventually drop the extrinsic candy reward. Incentives don't have to keep getting bigger, like bribes. It took a total of only twenty-five M & M candies for the boy to go to class alone. Soon he forgot all about the candy reward and found enough reward from the attention he earned discussing what he had learned in the class.

You have to be careful in using food as a reward or you may teach bad eating habits, so don't go overboard. But, we have to admit, food can be a powerful motivator. "Everybody who picks up and puts away twenty things gets a popsicle." You can't be handing out popsicles everytime you want something done, but if you were ready to have a treat time, why not have a short pick-up time first. In fact, stopping to pick up is a good habit to start. The progress chart called Ice-Cream Sundae, as shown on page 63, is a fun, longer-term incentive. Popcorn is also a good incentive. Keep a *sensible* balance; the leverage will be lost if you are doling out handfuls of sweets every time the child does something.

You may not have thought of it this way, but cooking has a food reward—eating. Washing dishes does not have the same appeal as mixing up a batch of chocolate chip cookies. Try including as much of the clean-up as possible with the preparation, where the incentive is. Besides, most bowls and pans are easier to wash right away unless they need soaking. It is easier to put away the salt, sugar, flour, and cinnamon one at a time, as each is used, than to wait until the end, when all the containers have been dusted with flour and everything needs to be wiped off. An incentive here might be to say that you can't eat until the preparation mess is cleaned up.

One school teacher in a small town formed an ice-cream club for good spellers and perfect-math-paper producers. A certain number of perfect papers merited an ice-cream treat: single scoop, double, or triple scoop; hot fudge sundae; or banana split. As the child earned the reward, the teacher drove him or her to the ice-cream shop for the one-to-one reward. You can see how easily parents could set up such an incentive plan for a desirable behavior or habit. It has a double reward of food and adult attention.

CHANCES

The Talbots, a family with five children, tried an incentive technique based on the "positive image campaign" used in a California school. Adapting this idea at home, Mrs. Talbot gave out chances for good behavior and helpfulness in the form of rectangular pieces of colored paper; one chance for fifteen minutes work, three chances for music practicing, and so forth. The child put his or her name on the chance and slipped it into a decorated box on the kitchen counter. At the end of the day, a drawing was held and the winner picked a reward from the "goodie box" (instant pudding, Twinkies, individual cereals, Snack Pack, peanuts, etc.). This may sound like it took a lot of time, but Mrs. Talbot claims it actually took less time—working with the positive meant less policing. After the drawing, the chance slips were taken from the box and saved. When a child had one hundred chances she earned a movie ticket. Mrs. Talbot said it was the best motivation system they had tried, because it offered immediate rewards for the positive behavior. The parents spent less time calling the children to do their work, practice music, or finish a job.

CHALLENGES

"Let's see who has the most seeds in their tangerine," challenged Bonnie one day in a desperate appeal to get her family to eat the tangerines. They preferred the no-seed navel oranges, but Bonnie couldn't throw out thirty pounds of tangerines just because they had seeds! Five years later, her children are still counting tangerine seeds—but, obviously, not the same thirty pounds. Be inventive with challenges.

The challenge: "Can I get dressed before the timer rings?" "How many diapers can I fold in ten minutes?" "Will I get the dishwasher emptied during this commercial break?" You may not believe this, but the McCullough kids have been known to get all their Saturday morning chores done during television commercials between cartoons. Children love to play Beat the Clock. The challenge should not be a person-against-person one because resentment can develop. There is enough rivalry between siblings without nurturing it. For example, if we tell Matt (five) and Becky (eight), "Let's see who can get dressed first," the one who loses will cry. It would be better to say, "Let's see who can be dressed before the timer rings in ten minutes," giving them both a chance to win. Another method that would instill cooperation may be to say, "As soon as the two of you get dressed and come together . . . ," leaving an option for them to help and encourage each other.

MONEY

Money can be used as an incentive, if you heed the same cautions that need to be used in other areas; with moderation and simplicity, and without escalation. Karen brought home twenty dollars' worth of nickles. Her husband had grown up in the South and wanted their children to start learning to say "yes sir," and "yes ma'am." Karen gave each child a nickle when he or she answered with the new responses—an immediate reward, better in this case than saving up points and giving the nickles out later. It worked. Three years later, the children are still answering "yes sir" and "yes ma'am."

If a child wants money for a special purchase, it can be enough motivation for him to try something new. When Wes wanted a dollar to go bowling, his mother offered it to him for scrubbing the kitchen floor, a task he had never tried, but he did it and was paid. On another occasion, when a choice of jobs was given, without pay (it was a family crisis to get ready for company), he chose to scrub the kitchen floor because he knew how. All of Chapter 10 deals with money and the child.

One mother used money as reward and consequence to train her preteens to pick up after themselves. She gave each child fifteen dimes in a baby-food jar. "This is your spending money for next weekend. Every time I pick up something of yours I get one of your dimes and you can have all the dimes left in your jar on Saturday." She set the jars in the kitchen window. The first week, Mom had enough to go out for Saturday breakfast. The next week her earnings would only buy a candy bar. The children insisted that to be fair, Mom and Dad should also have a jar of dimes, and if they could find something of Mom's or Dad's left out, the children could collect from the adults. Another family used a similar idea, with the family recreational allotment in the jars. The money left in each person's jar determined the amount he or she could spend for a restaurant dinner on Friday evening. (They normally went out as a family anyway. This was just a way of drawing attention to a new habit.)

Sue Monson used play money in her school classroom much like the Talbots used the chances, giving out work dollars for effort and accomplishment. The last ten minutes on Friday afternoon she held an auction for things like posters and bulletin board display items that weren't needed anymore at school. The kids loved it and liked to plan how to spend their "money." The same idea could be used at home just for fun. Wouldn't it be a thrill to get paid five hundred dollars for doing the dishes?

Don hides pennies and dimes under the bed, next to the radiator, and under the lamp to motivate and test how well his children clean. He got that idea from a sergeant in the Army. If the child usually receives an allowance, hide that amount in small coins throughout the child's room; if the room is thoroughly cleaned all the money should be found. Caution: no guarantee the child will clean as she hunts! The money might need to be marked with colored tape so it won't be confused with other money that could be in the room.

THE UNEXPECTED RESPONSE

An unexpected reaction by a parent can generate a shock effect in the child—and give the parent control. For example, when Judy's four children start to quarrel over the dishes, Judy stands up on the table with a wooden spoon in her hand and starts singing "Love at Home." (Who can fight with that going on?) An elderly schoolteacher, weighing about two hundred pounds, lays a great big kiss on any misbehaving fifth grader—works better than scolding, threats, or spanking. If you can't sleep at night, try dreaming up unexpected positive responses.

When one of Sue's third grade students started making weird, disruptive noises during a spelling test, Sue quickly said, "Oh, let's stop and listen. Here, Tom, stand up on the desk so we can see and hear you better. Now make those noises for us." This atypical response brought silence from Tom and put Sue back in control. At home an unexpected positive response can be helpful too. When Bobby starts moaning about doing the dishes, say, "Hey, Bobby, slow down. I want to write all those excuses on this paper. We'll number them and next time you can just refer to the number." Then begin writing down his complaints and excuses.

WATCH FOR THE RIGHT INCENTIVE

Sometimes, if you are watching, motivation opportunities will surface. One mother, whose teen-age son had extreme difficulty keeping his room clean, found a clue in her son's request for a good feather pillow. "Yes, son, you can have this pillow as long as you make your bed every day." On other occasions, the parents had tried offering him the moon without getting any improvement in the bedroom. Although the bedroom was a major problem, they didn't want to drive their son away from home by making it a constant issue. He still needed their adult parentship and the atmosphere of a loving home. Part of this incentive game is finding the right key. One day the boy forgot to make the bed and, without comment, the pillow was taken away. That day the boy made the bed when he got home from school, redeeming the pillow, and it didn't happen again. By this time, the boy had learned he could make the bed quickly and he liked it better that way. The incentive had helped overcome the hang-up. When he saw the bed was neatly made, he felt good, he knew it pleased his parents, and his self-esteem shot up.

Children want to succeed, but sometimes they need to know that their parents will help them with reminders, encouragement, and love. Being parents is not an easy game, and you're never sure that you have won.

Be aware of local or seasonal ideas that might trigger incentives or add interest. Little Sarah (two years) thought up the idea of the sock for a Dust Muppet and a rag was a Dinosaur Eater to eat (wipe) up a milk spill. One night, after hearing a chapter from *Pippi Longstocking,* five-year-old Mattie said, "I want to be a *thing finder.*" With that bit of interest, you could get a bucket or apron, pin a Thing Finder sign on him and put him to work cleaning under the sofa cushions. Add more fun to your family life with rewards and incentives.

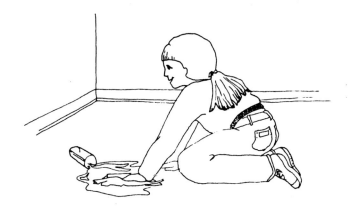

8: Providing Logical Consequences

No matter how exciting, how easy, fun, fair, and organized you have made the work, you must anticipate that your rules will be tested. And you should be ready by deciding now how your policies will be enforced. The outside world is filled with consequences. If you don't pay the phone bill, your phone service will be disconnected. When you walk on thin ice, you will fall through. Whether you are an adult or child, if you stick a nail in an electric outlet you will get shocked. These are natural consequences. Using natural laws as discipline wherever possible is most effective. When there isn't a natural consequence or it is too dangerous, logical consequences can be structured by the parent. Examples: "If you misuse the car, you turn in your keys." "When you cause a spill, whether on purpose or by accident, you clean it up." Learning to use consequences takes effort, so think ahead. Generally there are two types of logical consequences:

1. If a privilege is misused, it is withdrawn for a short time. (Could be car, radio, telephone, etc.)
2. If damage is done, the consequence should be to undo the damage as much as possible.

Using logical consequences can be extremely effective and save much frustration and friction. Structuring safe consequences increases respect for rules. This type of discipline keeps you on the level of teacher rather than executioner. Taking time to determine the consequence may mean leaving the scene until you can logically think it through. Be sure you have a good feeling about the direction you are pursuing. You are entitled to feel it is right for your family. Nothing works for everyone. If used with anger or for retaliation these ideas can cause damage to the child.

Before you act, ask yourself these questions about the consequence:

_____ Is it reasonable?
_____ Is it enforceable?
_____ Is it consistent with nurturous care?
_____ Is it too powerful?
_____ Is there anger, resentment, or retaliation associated with issuing this consequence?
_____ Is it clearly related to the offense?

Is the consequence reasonable? You want this consequence to be a logical, rational result of the child's misjudgment. In a survey, we asked children what happened when they did not do their work and they gave the following answers:

"Still have to do them later."

"I don't get paid."

"She yells at me."

"Bitch, bitch, bitch."

"No TV."

"Grounded."

Do you think these kids changed their performance? Carefully think through the relationship between the behavior and the consequence. Stopping television privileges has nothing to do with leaving the drawers in a bureau open, but it could be related to the cluttered area in front of the television. Shawn, an eight-year-old, repeatedly left his dresser drawers open. It made the room look messy and it was dangerous for his younger brother, who slept next to the dresser. Rather than restrict television privileges or issue a paddling, which had nothing to do with his neglectful habit, his mother calmly said, "Shawn, you seem to be having such a hard time keeping these drawers closed, I guess you need a training session. I want you to practice opening and closing these drawers ten times. Watch me first." It was so ridiculous that they were both laughing before he was finished. He got the point, and it worked better than angrily dumping the contents on the floor.

Another time, when Shawn and his younger brother Tim were watching television on Saturday morning, they got out three puzzles and five games. They watched the ball game and dropped the newspapers on the floor, and older sisters watched a movie and left socks and shoes. No one seemed to notice the mess in front of the set or made a motion to pick up any of it. Before dinner, Mom announced, "Since you don't care enough to pick up a little in the family room, you will lose the privilege of using it and watching TV." Since it was a family tradition to watch the Muppets at six-thirty on Saturday night, they all devoted five minutes to the room. The consequence was related to the offense.

One mother said, "All right, you guys, if you don't hang up

the towels, you don't get any," and took them all out of the bathroom. She stood firm on the consequence—they had to dry off with toilet tissue and tiptoe to the bedroom naked. Was the consequence reasonable? Did they learn what she wanted them to? Maybe. It might make the point as a one-time lesson, or there might be another consequence that could be used—but it's hard to think of one. That's what makes this consequence business so hard to deal with. Maybe a large note. Perhaps a four-week incentive. Most parents would just nag, yell, or withhold privileges indiscriminately. Try offering them five M & M candies—a fifteen-year-old would get a kick out of that.

One father and mother, embarrassed and upset because their eight-year-old boy set off the fire alarm at school, told him, "You are a bad boy. You don't deserve to have anything." They put all his toys out on the sidewalk for the neighborhood kids to take. The parents were very inconsistent: lenient one day, too restrictive the next. This boy's action was a plea for help—he did not receive it.

Back to the question: Is the consequence reasonable? If you are angry or mad, you are too likely to retaliate rather than correct. Send the child to the "time-out" corner, box, or room—whatever you use—to give you time to think clearly and let the child get control of his feelings too. Then ask him why he is in the "time-out" spot, so you know that he understands why he is there. You might get some good ideas by asking him what his discipline should be, if it is needed. And don't forget to ask him how he could handle the situation in a better way next time. If he has learned from the mistake, it gives him positive reinforcement for future change. Sometimes the reasonable consequence is to go back and undo the damage as much as possible. One father uses this in verbal expressions so the child has practice using the correct response. He can be heard to say, "Those words in that tone of voice are not acceptable. Please say it again in a nicer way." The child then gives an appropriate answer that meets with Dad's approval: "That's much better."

If your child forgets a school book or assignment, do you run it up to the school? Sometimes it is best to let the natural consequence occur at school, so the child learns to stop and ask herself before going out the door, "Do I have everything?" She is learning to be aware, taking time to think it through, and being responsible for herself. On the other side, one mother said, "My kids are good at helping me in a spot, so when they make an occasional mistake, I don't mind helping them out." We don't want the child to become so dependent on us that she doesn't develop a sense of responsibility, but we want to temper our reactions with understanding and reason.

Is this consequence enforceable? Be sure to ask yourself this before you let the words out of your mouth—you may be punishing yourself or have to back down from the "promise." Don't threaten to leave the child home unless you intend to (and it's safe). Do not ground a six-year-old to his bedroom and then leave, expecting older sister to enforce the restriction. Turning off the television for a week may punish you more than the children if your schedule is too busy to help them find new things to do.

Fay said her seventeen-year-old son used her good sewing scissors to cut wire. The logical consequence was for him to take them and pay to have them sharpened. He had the money and a car and could do this. But the consequence for a nine-year-old would be different. John was trying to teach his children to turn off the lights when they left the bedroom. Each time he found a light on and no one in the room, he unscrewed one of the bulbs until there were no lights. They lost the privilege of light for one night. The first time a lamp or radio was left on, John would unplug it. The effort to replug it was a reminder to the child. The second offense meant it was taken away for one day; the third offense, for two days. After three times, he asked them to pay part of the utility bill. Another parent charged his children a nickle every time the light was left on. Consider the parent who gave a Lifesaver candy for turning the light out—it made them stop and think about it even more than the nickle.

Logical consequences: If you track grease in on the carpet, you shampoo the carpet. If walking around in your stocking feet makes holes in your socks, you mend them or buy the next pair. When your clothes come through the laundry wrong side out, you get them back that way—or you don't get them washed until they have been turned. The director of the Pocatello choir had an enforceable consequence—a fifty-cent fine for being late back to the bus—devised to cut down on delays on the concert tour. The monies collected bought dinner the last night on the road.

Is this consequence enforceable? "You must take the trash out before the end of the day (midnight)." At 11:55 P.M. Dad, in a matter-of-fact way, woke up the daughter to take out the trash—a one-time lesson. Another interesting limit is "This must be done before you eat next."

Requiring a repayment for unnecessary service from a parent may greatly reduce the work. If a child doesn't finish a chore and it can't be left until he gets home, he must do a make-up chore such as sweeping the porch. This works especially well for redeeming an only coat—which may mean reducing the coat collection. When clean clothes are thrown into the laundry rather than hung up, have the child wash those clothes by hand. To make certain the child knows what brought about the consequence, include a time to talk. Asking him to restate the broken rule is one of the most effective tricks. It removes misunderstandings and reinforces his memory for next time. It needs to be done in a kind, matter-of-fact way, not to "make him eat crow."

EIGHT O'CLOCK PICK-UP

Carolyn discovered a natural consequence that worked wonders. The incident that motivated Carolyn and her husband, Bob, to try this program was the mess they came home to one night. Books, toys, clothes, towels and dishes were everywhere. Rather than wake everyone in their anger, they laid out a plan. The next morning they explained to the children, "We will go through the house twice a day at eight o'clock. Anything left out in the general living areas will be put in the Extra-Service Box and will have to be redeemed with a chore sometime before Saturday at noon. Consider yourselves warned." That night, Carolyn and Bob picked up twelve things. Next morning, when the children noticed the Extra-Service Box sitting in a conspicuous place on top of the refrigerator, they were all curious about who had things in the box. "What do I need to do for you, Mom, to earn back my shoes?" "Wipe off the TV screen" was the answer.

Carolyn had unsuccessfully tried using a similar technique before, where she would pick up an item left out at any time. This was asking for perfection from the child and the parent had to stand guard all the time. It was unenforceable. Her real purpose was not to make the child perfect but to get him or her to notice and put away their own things. She did not mind so much that things were left out in temporary spots once in a while, but it angered her when those temporary spots became permanent and the child never noticed the item until it was needed several days later. For example, one of her sons had three coats. He would go to the closet every time he needed a coat and only when there was not a coat in the closet would he think about where he could have left them.

This time, as Carolyn used this behavior modification technique, it was easier to be consistent with the consequence because it only happened twice a day. She also watched for chances to reinforce the desired behavior when a child did pick up something: "Becky is saving herself an extra-service chore by picking up her shoes.'' An important ingredient for changing a habit is giving positive recognition for the desired action.

The evening of the second day, the fifteen-year-old could be seen picking up a whole arm load as she headed toward her bedroom. Success! It was working. This young lady was very involved in school activities but was especially careless at home. It was this teen who put her dad's shoes in the box because they were out after eight o'clock and declared he would have to do her an extra chore. The fourth morning was Saturday. As the eleven-year-old boy appeared for breakfast, he noticed the service box and started checking to see if he had to redeem anything. ''What do I need to do to redeem my coat, Mom?'' Carolyn had him take the newspapers out to the garage. This young man not only redeemed his own items, but everyone else's too. Then he proudly took each item to the owner, telling about his generosity. Carolyn's eight-year-old daughter had a spurt of energy while her mother was gone, and emptied the dish drainer and washed a sinkful of dishes. ''Did you like the way I helped out? Does that mean I have redeemed something ahead of time?'' Success again! She was noticing things that needed to be done without being told.

This eight o'clock pick-up was used by Carolyn every day for several weeks and then she let it die because the children were much improved at picking up after themselves. Three months later, she used it again for a few days to reinforce the principle. Why did the eight o'clock pick-up work?

1. The children were mature enough to understand.
2. The eight o'clock rounds were easier to enforce than the ''all the time'' rule.
3. The Extra-Service Box was left out where it could be seen.
4. Redemption chores were kept very, very simple—less than five minutes (child's time) and chores that were not normally theirs.
5. Special efforts were made to give lots of positive atten-

tion when the children picked up and put things away at other times.

6. A gentle, one-time reminder was often given before the parent's rounds were made.

7. The child's things left out in his own bedroom did not count; rather, they were treated with the daily pick-up chore by the child in the room and on Saturday when the bedroom was thoroughly cleaned.

Is the consequence consistent with nurturous care? It is typically stated that the consequence for being late to dinner or not coming when called is to go without eating. Withholding food, according to Selma H. Fraiberg, who wrote *The Magic Years,* does not make a good punishment, especially for the young child, because it "touches off a psychological chain reaction." The child's mind starts "fantasies in which the parents are monsters who will even let a child go hungry and the whole episode produces such outrage that the intended lesson is lost." Then what will we do with the child who is late for dinner? Let her eat standing up or alone. She can eat from what is left and do her own clean-up. If the child is too young to clean up, she is certainly too young to understand no dinner. Try another technique to teach the lesson. Examine how the child was called. Was a warning time given? What about the child that is slow or dawdles at meals? Same thing. Go ahead and eat. When everyone else is finished, clean up. Either leave her alone to finish and have her clean up her own dishes or tell her meal time is over and take the food away. The secret is not to allow in-between-meal snacks. No need for constant nagging during a meal. The child will learn to eat when the food is available and not hold out for possible goodies later.

Fraiberg goes on to say, "Whether any method of discipline works will depend upon the fundamental relationship of a child to his parents." When nothing works, "the answer does not lie in a fancier technique of discipline, but an examination of the parent-child relationship." Children can be so ingenious in their techniques to get attention and to manipulate adults that it isn't fair that adults do not have the same natural instincts for knowing how to handle children. We have to band together and pool all our ideas to find successful ways to deal with their misbehaviors. Your own parents or grandparents may have valuable advice. Talk to others, read all you can, and take an active roll in parent-teacher groups and church groups for support in your efforts to raise a child.

"If the punishment is excessive, that is exceeds a child's tolerance, it will have no beneficial effects and will only feed the child's sense of being unjustly treated and give rise to hostile and vengeful feelings," continued Fraiberg. One father insisted, "If you kids can't do the dishes without fighting, I guess you need more practice," and took down every dish in the cupboard to be washed. Did they learn the intended lesson of no fighting or were they resentful to each other as well as angry at Dad? Another dad said, "If you kids are going to fight while doing dishes, you will have to take turns washing them all alone. It is a privilege to do them together."

One teacher sent students out of the classroom for forty-five minutes every time they answered a question without raising their hands. Did it teach the child to raise her hand before blurting out the answer? No, the child quit answering altogether. The same thing happened at one home where the mother sent the two daughters to their own bedrooms for an hour each time they started arguing. After three days of this consequence, they quit bickering, but they also quit playing together. The teacher and mother made two mistakes: 1) They neglected to positively reinforce the desired behavior along with the consequence for the wrong. 2) The time-out was too long. Five or ten minutes in the time-out spot is usually enough for the child to get control. Pam Brace and Peggy Jones tell of a fantastic consequence their mother used. "If you are fighting, you must wash windows, one on each side, until you are smiling at each other."

Is the consequence too powerful? You are careful when allowing natural consequences to be the result of a bad decision. Certainly you are not going to let the child be hit by a car just because she made a bad decision about going into the street. When structuring logical consequences, be just as careful not to let it damage the child psychologically or socially. Yes, it can hurt a little, but destroy self-image or hope—no! For example: A story was printed in a newspaper about a ten-year-old boy who was given a ten-speed bike for his birthday along with some instructions about its use and care. "No riding on the highway and always put it away in the garage." After *one* warning for leaving the bike out, the father sold it and kept the money. The young man cried. In this instance, he decided to earn the money to buy a new one and then took proper care of it, so it was reported as a success story. But in most instances a ten-year-old would not have opportunities to earn enough money to buy another bike. It would not have taught him responsibility; rather, bitterness would most likely have resulted. If the punishment, even though logical, is too severe and exceeds the child's tolerance, it will do more harm than good. If you park your car in front of a No Parking sign, you'll probably get a ticket or the car may even be towed away, but would the mayor sell your car? No. What other logical consequence could be structured for this ten-year-old who is still struggling with the habit of leaving things out? It might be "impounded" for a day or two. A way could be set for him to "earn" it back. Making consequences too severe can be just as damaging as protecting the child from all consequences.

Let's take a money example. "If you break something, you are responsible and should pay for it." But to what degree is the child liable? If he pulls up the neighbor's tulips, you could provide a way for him to earn the money to replace the bulbs. What if he breaks the neighbor's car window? One set of parents held a nine-year-old boy financially liable when he unknowingly sold the radial tires instead of the snow tires to a man answering their newspaper ad. They decided to withhold his two dollar a week allowance for three years. It may have sounded very logical to the parents, but the punishment was too severe and the blame belonged with the parents.

One teacher told his fifth graders that every time a paper was turned in late, that student would miss recess for a week. He had decided it was time to teach responsibility to prepare them for junior high school. He stuck to his threat, no exceptions. To the conscientious student whose two-year-old brother tore up her paper, the consequence was devastating. The students who didn't care very much gave up even trying because two, three, or four weeks without recess is forever. Suppose he had made the consequence less powerful—perhaps missing one recess? When these students got to junior high, they found it wasn't as he had said anyway; the teachers just deducted ten percent off the grade of the paper for every day the paper was late.

If the consequence is too stern, change it. Good consequences build acceptance, bad ones build resentment. Another example: Mom and Dad came home from work to find their two sons had not cleaned up the kitchen, which was their assignment. "This is too unsanitary to even cook or eat in." They turned around, left, and ate out, leaving the boys to fend for themselves. This happened three days in a row and on the fourth day, the kitchen was clean when they got home from work. Would this technique have worked in most families? No. The boys would have fixed peanut-butter-and-jelly sandwiches and watched television or might have gone to a friend's house. We need to know more about this circumstance. Could the kids clean up the kitchen by themselves? Who made the mess? Was it an accumulation from the weekend? Do those boys need more help in knowing how to conquer a monstrous mess? Is there an incentive that could be structured, like the Ice-Cream Sundae chart, to reward positive behavior? (It wouldn't cost as much as going out to eat for three nights.) These parents had the correct principle in mind—"If *this* is not completed, we can't move on to *this*"—but perhaps the boys needed more training in accomplishing the first. On the other hand, maybe the parents were right; that the boys were just being lazy and needed to be taught a lesson.

Is there any anger, resentment, or retaliation associated with imposing this consequence? If the child neglects her morning chores, is the parent to go get her from school and bring her home to do them? One principal said, "If a mother should come after a child in that circumstance, she is usually mad, her efforts have not been consistent at home, all of a sudden everything gets to her, and she is ready to take it out on the child. It will just be another negative experience." Such a consequence would be logical only if the parents had been very, very consistent at home before this time—teaching, training, following up, and giving positive reinforcement—and very few are like that. So, what is the parent to do when the child skips out to school without taking care of home assignments? If the job has to be done and can't wait, a redeeming chore would be required; otherwise save it until the child gets home. The best time to catch the slip is before the child goes to school, perhaps by concentrating more on morning supervision for a time. The parent who insists the work be done before school has the natural consequence of being late to motivate the child to hurry. Maybe there are good reasons for not finishing morning chores. What happens if you don't get your bed made in the morning? You make it when you get home. Does your neighbor come over and give you heck? One mother decided the child's chores would be saved until after school if they weren't finished in the morning. But she noticed that when she had the children do their left-over chores right after school, it took so long there wasn't any free time for play—a necessary outlet after the restrictions and pressures of school. It wasn't all that important to do it immediately, but at five o'clock, play time was over, television turned off and *everyone* worked on the chores for the day. Her logical time limit was that chores have to be done before dinner, and then she made sure this hour was reserved for the chores. Try to keep consequences fair and friendly.

Is this consequence related to the offense? Many adults

withhold allowance as a punishment for uncompleted chores or bad behavior. This depends on your logic for giving money. If it is given as a paycheck for doing certain tasks, when the job isn't done don't give the money. But if you issue allowance as a tool to provide experience in handling money and teach wise buying habits, and assume each child will take part in the maintenance and upkeep of the inside and outside of your home as part of their family responsibility, then you won't want to use the allowance as a disciplinary rod. One couple whose children are paid for jobs at home, charge ten cents for each reminder. "I am reminding you to sweep the stairs." The prompting is recorded on paper with time and date. When pay day comes, the written note is given to the child with the rest of his wage. Keeping a written record and following through make their system work.

The very day Bonnie began writing about this topic of logical consequences, she arrived home at 10 P.M. to find her five-year-old, who was supposed to be in bed at eight, still up. He was sent to bed. Mom, Dad, older brother and sister were served chocolate chip ice cream with chocolate sauce. He was crushed. "Can't I have any?" "No, because you didn't go to bed when you were told to," was the reply. Ten minutes later he came back into the room, where they were watching the news. "Mom, if I had gone to bed when I was supposed to, I wouldn't have had ice cream either." Smart kid. The reason she gave for the punishment had the wrong relationship to the offense—the child could see the unfairness and the lesson was lost. (But he still didn't get the ice cream.)

The first type of logical consequence was, "If a privilege is misused, it is lost for a time." One young mother of three- and five-year-olds found when her children went to play in the family room, they would pull out everything. It was so bad, there wasn't a place to walk. They wouldn't put any of it away unless Mom was helping. They were playing with Mommie, not with the toys. They enjoyed the time she spent cleaning up and chiding them about the mess. Part of the solution was to separate the toys that had been all together in large toy boxes into smaller categories in bags and boxes. Then she put more than half of them away, to be rotated. Changing the circumstance helped to change their behavior. It also helped this mother to know that a young child cannot mentally grasp abstract concepts like cleanliness and needs much parental patience and help until at least six or seven years old. It was better to simplify the circumstance until they could manage more items.

Let reasonable consequences happen as long as they aren't too powerful or cause physical or mental harm to the child. There will be some hurt and sadness. One father councils with his children and asks, "What did you learn from your mistake?" If he feels the child has learned from the experience, "that is enough punishment." The parent's job is to support and reassure: "You can do it," "I am with you." There are some problems the child must battle himself. Sometimes we have to learn to say no to the pleadings of today, in order to say yes to the happiness of tomorrow.

Children are tender. When discipline is necessary, show increased love soon afterward, otherwise the child may begin to see you as his enemy. Keep the consequences fair and related to the offense. Don't just blow up and say, "You can't go to the birthday party" or deny whatever the next privilege is to be. Ask yourself, "Is this the way I would like someone to talk to me?" "Is this how I would talk to a friend's child?" Keep it simple so the child can understand the association between the act and the consequence. Give a warning when possible: "You understand the consequence of this behavior will be...." Good consequences teach self-control, fairness, and respect for rules.

9: Organizing the Bedroom

One of the biggest dilemmas for parents is what can be done about the child's bedroom. If we leave the care of the room totally to the child, he or she may decide not to clean it, and learn to accept it messy—which is hard on the child's self-image (and future spouse or roommates). If the parent cleans the room for the child all of the time, the child will learn to like it clean, but expect someone else to clean it. Neither of these attitudes is healthy. Adopt the theory that it is better to help children with their rooms so they learn to like order and feel good about themselves, than to withdraw, close the door, and allow them to live in a mess.

Assume that children like a room to be clean. You can tell because as soon as a room has been cleaned the children want to play there. If we have just finished cleaning the kitchen, someone wants to make cookies. After straightening the family room, they want to start a puzzle or bring out the building blocks. Although children like the good feeling of living in a clean room, they are often too immature to know how to keep it that way. Adult assistance is needed to teach, motivate, and insist that a certain minimum level of cleanliness be maintained.

The first thing to do to help the child organize the bedroom is to evaluate the reasons for the problem. Take thirty minutes, go sit down on the *floor* of your child's bedroom, and brainstorm causes and possible solutions. (Have a tablet and pencil with you.) Look at the room from the child's point of view— that's why you are sitting on the floor. In evaluating the room, look for ways to (1) cut down the quantity of items to a manageable number for the age and maturity of the child, (2) arrange the room to make it as easy as possible for the child to pick up and clean, and (3) make a definite place for everything in the room.

Cut down the quantity. Consider the structure and physical limitations of the room. Is there too much in the room? If four boys are sharing one room, it is obvious that each can not have as many things as a single child. Is there some way part of the child's belongings could be stored elsewhere? Even better, does he need all of these things? Maybe getting rid of part of them would simplify his life. It is sometimes easier for parents to keep their bedroom in order because they have other places to store treasures and equipment, but the child may be keeping all of his belongings in his bedroom. Given his immaturity, asking him to go clean his bedroom is about like telling the parent to go clean K-Mart after a giant end-of-season sale. Perhaps you could help this child store part of his things and discard another part of them. After it has been out of sight for a while, he may realize he really doesn't need it and it could be disposed of at a garage sale or given to Santa's Workshop. Asking yourself these questions can be very enlightening, as one mother whose twenty-three-year-old daughter had an atrocious-looking bedroom discovered. She had enough stuff crammed in her bedroom to fill a house—wedding gifts left from a broken marriage and *all* the equipment for a new baby. Once the problem was identified, they worked together to box up most of the things and store them for a time.

Check the room arrangement.   While you are sitting there on the floor, look for ways the room could be arranged to make it easier for a little person to manage. What about the bed? Are the sheets, blankets, and bedspread manageable, or are they the ones adults think cute or pretty, but that are hard for a child to make up neatly? Perhaps a bedspread with long, horizontal cording that marks the side edges of the bed or a design showing how far over the bed the bedspread should be is better. Some children have a washable quilt that can easily be pulled up rather than having a top sheet and bedspread with it. The child can make it by just crawling up to the head of the bed, pulling up the cover, smoothing it, and slithering out. If you have enough room, pull the bed away from the wall for easier bed making. As you are looking for ways to make the room arrangement easier, ask, "Can the child hang up his own coat and robe?" If not, maybe hooks would be easier than hangers. You will probably want a wastebasket and some kind of clothes hamper in the room. Shoe boxes in the drawers make terrific dividers to separate socks, underwear, belts, and pajamas. As you sit on the floor evaluating, you will come up with some good ideas, but don't forget to ask for the child's opinions, too.

Create a place for everything.   A child needs adult help doing this. Go through the following list and check items that still need a resting place. The two-year-old's bedroom will look a bit different than the seventh grader's, and the child in a room by himself will have more flexibility than children sharing a room. Make these suggestions fit your circumstances.

☐ Is there a place to sleep that the child can manage?

☐ Is there a place for hanging clean clothes? Normally, this would be a closet. Is the rod low enough? If you don't want to alter the closet permanently, hang a broom stick from the higher rod with ropes. The younger child can pull clean clothes off the hangers, but it is a more advanced skill to put them back on a hanger. At this age, they are usually only wearing clothes for one day and then putting them in the laundry, but what about the robe, coats, and sweaters that don't need washing every time? Perhaps hooks would be best. Some children don't need a closet because everything they wear can be folded.

☐ Is there a place for out-of-season clothes and clothes not yet grown into? So often, because the child doesn't need all the closet space for current clothes, we hang the out-of-size and out-of-season clothes in the closet too, but this can create managing problems. Try boxing up these extra clothes in sturdy fruit boxes and storing them in the top of the closet or some other area like the laundry room.

☐ Is there a place for shoes and boots? Will their place be under the bed? Is there unused space at the end of the closet that could be fitted with little shelves?

☐ Is there a place for dirty clothes? You would be surprised how many adults expect children to carry their dirty clothes to a central clothes hamper in the bathroom or downstairs to the wash area every time they undress. Try putting a container like a hamper, large wastebasket or box covered with wallpaper conveniently *in* the room or closet.

☐ Is there a place for folded clean clothes? Usually the child has drawers for clean clothing. What about hats and gloves? Perhaps a dish pan on the closet shelf or hooks by the back door. Some families have a special tradition of putting the pajamas away under the bed pillow or in a zip-up stuffed animal. Help the child remember the system of organization by labeling the shelves and drawers. If you have many children in your family, organize every chest of drawers the same way, such as: top drawer, treasures; second drawer, pajamas, undies, and socks; third drawer, pants and shirts; and fourth drawer, junk. One more tip: Make it an annual tradition to clean out the drawers by using the wrapping paper from the child's birthday gifts to line the drawers. The excitement of Christmas can motivate children to clean closets and drawers. "Let's make room for new gifts. Can we give some of these to a family in need?"

☐ Is there a place for trash?

☐ Is there a place for books? Perhaps the answer is a headboard with a bookcase, a set of brick-and-board shelves, or shelves in the closet. If you want the child to read for pleasure, have a place for books in the bedroom.

☐ Is there a table or desk? It is especially important, after the child has entered middle school or junior high, to have a place to do homework; however, it could be done in another designated area in your home.

☐ Is there a place to put school books and pending homework?

☐ Is there a place to keep finished papers and reports? Maybe a real file cabinet or just a box in the closet is the solution.

☐ Is there a place to keep toys? Except for large toys, toy boxes are the worst possible storage. Every time the children want a toy, they dump the whole box and make a big mess. Games and puzzles with many pieces seldom get back together after being dumped in a toy box. Consider

separating the games, building blocks, and puzzles into bags (net bags like the ones grapefruit come in are terrific), or boxes. Put a large rubber band around the box in case it should be dropped, so everything doesn't come out. Buy inexpensive sewing elastic and tack the two ends together to make your own sturdy elastic bands. Hooks in the closet, a pegged mug rack, peg board, or game tree (like coat tree but with hooks all the way down the pole) can hold these toy bags. For stuffed animals, a suspension pole could be set in the corner, holes drilled for hooks, and each animal, with a ribbon around its neck, hung from the pole. Or vertically hang a long, two-inch wooden dowel from a plant hook in the ceiling. Screw cup hooks into the wood on which to hang toys. Secure a fishing net between two walls in a corner of the room as a hammock for dolls and animals.

☐ Is there a place for display? Little things that are important to the child need a place, especially if there are younger siblings who might ruin them. A simple knickknack shelf or a corner shelf might be the solution. If there are more items than will fit neatly, rotate them. A bulletin board or clothes line along a wall could be used to display posters or art papers and reports. There are pictures and mementoes that are nice to put in a scrapbook to be shown to future generations. Guide the child in knowing what to keep. Old, blurred, or dark pictures have no value. Label pictures with names and dates for easy identification.

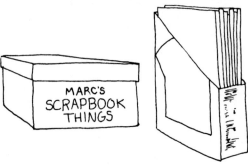

☐ Are there other organizing tools? A mirror, calendar, pencil holder, and pin cushion help a child get organized.

Even though this is quite a long list, you, as parent, will find it will help your child keep things to a minimum so the child can manage them. Don't let hobbies and collections get out of hand. It may be necessary to re-evaluate your holiday and birthday giving or have a discussion with grandparents.

SET LIMITS

The places you have created to put things can carry an automatic limit. A dish pan or box for school papers is a limit. When the box is full, the child goes through the papers, keeping only the favorites. After storing things for awhile, some of the initial emotional attachment is gone and it is easier for the child to discard them. A bulletin board and knickknack shelf are limiting. When they are full, some of the papers or hobby items need to be stored.

Another important limit to consider is clothing. How often do you wash? Every other day? Once a week? Count the number of days between washings, add a couple, and that could be the limit on how many clothes are out. So often we keep two or three times that many clothes in the closet or chest and it complicates efforts to keep the room clean. Many of the clothes are never worn. We tend to hang as many clothes in the closet as the rod will hold rather than setting the limit on the number the child can manage. Perhaps you can rotate part of them. Some people find it best to keep out-of-season or out-of-fit clothes in fruit boxes in the top of the closet or under the bed. It is so hard to clean with *more*, even when there is space available. Involve your child in learning to manage a few things well. When a child isn't wearing a piece of clothing, suggest possibilities of matching it with other clothes. If they don't like an article of clothing, don't complicate life; just take it out.

Limits also need to be set for toys. Think about a rotation system, leaving some of the toys out on the toy shelves for a week or two and then rotating them with different ones that have been stored elsewhere. Young children find old toys carry the freshness of new toys after they have been out of sight for a time.

HELP THE CHILD MAKE
THE ROOM ATTRACTIVE

Add something new from time to time—it sparks interest. Give a new set of bed sheets or a bucket of paint for a birthday present. Just changing the furniture around when cleaning gives a feeling of newness and motivates the child to keep it clean for a few days. The child's bedroom doesn't have to have *everything* new or look like a magazine picture, but a change gives a boost to the child.

DO NOT THROW AWAY A CHILD'S
BELONGINGS WITHOUT ASKING

One mother said she has her seven-year-old son's bedroom under control. While he is at school, she goes through his things, throws out the junk, and cleans the room. To do it *for* him is only a temporary solution. It is not teaching him the skill of managing his possessions; he needs practice at letting go of things, at making those decisions. Heaven forbid if that child hasn't changed before he gets to be an adult, and worse yet, if he should marry one of our daughters! Set up limits in the child's bedroom and then guide him in making decisions about what to keep and what to eliminate. After the child is five or six, include him in throw-out decisions. One Air Force family that moved about every two years had the motto "If it hasn't been used since the last move, out it goes." Even when you have the space, you are not doing the child a favor by saving everything, as learned by a young couple who just moved into their first home. It was a small, two-bedroom bungalow, just right for them and their new baby. But the man's parents drove up with a full trailer to deliver. They had saved *every* toy and piece of clothing he had ever owned as a boy—giant model airplanes, an eight-foot soap-box racer, and so forth. The couple's solution was to build a garage. Stop and think. Just because your child owns and likes something now, that doesn't mean he wants to carry it around with him for the rest of his life. Guide the child in keeping a few treasures and turning loose of the other things after their season of interest.

HELP THE CHILD
CLEAN THE BEDROOM

A messy room for several days signals a need for parental help in cleaning and organizing. Most, although not all, children can handle their own bedrooms by age fourteen, but even after that age, they occasionally enjoy parental assistance. At about five or six years of age, when children start school and when they get more involved with friends, they start collecting more things, they receive nicer gifts that last longer, and they begin having trouble keeping the room clean. At this time, there is a great need for parental consistency. The parent need not insist that the child's room get forty-nine points on a fifty-point inspection sheet every day; very few adults, even, live that way. Help the child do a little minimum maintenance (pick up, make bed, take care of clothing) every day, and give the room a good cleaning, with vacuuming and dusting, once a week, maybe on Friday afternoon or Saturday morning. This tidy atmosphere is good for the child's self-image, it says "I am neat" and it pleases Mom and Dad. This attitude doesn't bind the child down to the perfection of always having to keep everything put away. There is much more to life than a clean

house, but a tidy atmosphere frees one in many ways to do other things, especially fun, creative things.

Help the child learn a cleaning system and divide the cleaning into small categories so that he can *see* progress. Children are capable of making a bigger mess than they can clean up; cleaning up is a more advanced skill. Have them start with the biggest thing first. Ask, "What is the biggest thing in your bedroom?" (Probably the bed.) "Let's clean if off first and make it." After the bed is made, both parent and child can see progress—a measurable success. What is the second biggest category that needs to be picked up? Perhaps the books or dirty clothes. Sometimes it is fun at this point to pick things up by color, "Now let's pick up everything that is red" and move on through other colors.

Take the attitude that this is the child's room and he or she is the manager, and the parent is the "consultant." Don't be afraid to ask "What would you like me to do?" but leave the child in charge. What you are after is more *in*dependence, not dependence. Continue guiding the child with the cleaning. It is more rewarding to do a complete pick-up *before* digging into the real cleaning procedures like dusting, washing windows, or straightening drawers. When the energy starts to wane, there will be something to *show* progress and motivate to completion. The theory is to work from outside to inside areas. If room cleaning is too unpleasant or takes too long, the child will procrastinate the next cleaning for an even longer time, a self-defeating cycle because the mess will be worse.

Encouragement and positive statements are the major reasons for the parent being with the child during cleaning periods. Point out the progress by comparing with the beginning mess, but don't turn the clean room into a moral issue. Do not say, "You are a bad girl when your room is messy." Also point out progress by saying, "See how nice the books look when they are all on the shelf!" or "Just closing the closet door makes quite a difference, doesn't it?" or "It's more fun to play in this clean room" or "Doesn't it make you feel good inside to have this all done?" or "We're halfway finished."

The two-point method for putting clothes in a hamper can be lots of fun and motivate your children to pick up. If the garment goes into the hamper when tossed, with nothing sticking out, you get two points. Instead of starting Lecture Number Thirty-eight about clothes all over the floor, just pick up a sock, toss it in the hamper, and announce, "I get two points." Most children pick up on this very quickly and want points too, and try to make the basket. From then on, the parent keeps score as the child picks up the clothes. If the item is hanging over the edge, only one point is given. (This is a method of giving immediate positive verbal rewards after each effort.) As a parent, you won't mind losing three-to-ten at this game because you are really the winner; the child has picked up the clothes, as you intended in the first place. The child will probably carry on the game even when the parent isn't there to prompt it, and putting clothes in the hamper will become a habit. Sometimes this little game works for Mom and Dad's clothes, too.

Learning to keep the bedroom neat can be a giant time-saving habit, redeemable throughout life. By following the five principles listed on the 7,500 Minute Certificate, one can save thirty minutes a day. A big payoff for daily effort!

7,500 Minute Certificate

Valid to bearer only if the following rules are followed:

1. Keep your room simple. Make a place for everything.
2. Store the things you are not using and the clothes you are not wearing.
3. Keep most accessible space for most-used items.
4. Make your bed first thing every day.
5. No halfway spots. Put it away while in hand.
6. Give your room a five-minute pick-up every day.

Certificate renewable every year of your life. Value is in time saved to do things you want to do.

What about the child who is very, very messy? It might help to know that only one child in five is born neat; the rest have to be taught. It will take patience and, even though it sounds discouraging, you may have to stick with helping the young child clean for several years, not just weeks. Carefully look for the possible cause of the problem, because it could be that the room is only a symptom of other problems. At about twelve years of age, some children go through a typical stage when they rebel about keeping up the bedroom. Go back and ask yourself these questions: Are there more things in the room than the child can manage? Am I giving positive verbal rewards? Is the child lacking in skill? Maybe it is the adult attention the child is seeking and this is the child's way of getting it. Don't use the haunting phrase "If you can't keep your bedroom clean now, how can you handle a whole house?" You could be building future failure. Keep trying, never give up, but don't nag or threaten. Continue looking for the incentive that will motivate now.

Sue Monson found a formal inspection sheet for older children helpful in establishing a clear standard and teaching exactly what was expected. She took the military approach one Friday in a desperate attempt to improve the bedrooms. After making a surprise check of each bedroom, she posted the scores on the doors. The "notice" included points awarded for each area of the room with comments like "Better luck next time!" and "You can only go up from here!" The scores showed the rooms were a mess. Of the fifty possible points, Mom and Dad scored the highest, a whopping fifteen points. The inspection sheet (see example that follows) taught everyone two things: to know the standard required and to take notice of the dirt and clutter. Since the children had not been at home when the surprise check was made, it brought on a lively discussion—a new approach to "go clean your room." When Sue told the children they could inspect their parents' room, they squealed and began planning to play the role as the toughest sergeants around, making the project seem fair and acceptable.

With the chart, the inspection could be completed in five minutes. The exact time of each upcoming inspection was

BEDROOM CHECK

50 Possible Points

Each category is worth 0–4 points. The best job receives the highest number of points. If 40 points or more are earned, a special treat will be given. If not, you may reschedule an inspection or plan to upgrade the score the next time.

Room __JANE'S__

Date _____

		Surprise 5/16	11 A.M. 5/17	2 P.M. 5/18	11 A.M. 5/24			
0–4	Bed made	0	4	4	4			
0–4	Under bed clean	0	0	4	4			
0–4	Drawers neat (2 checked)	2	2	3	4			
0–4	Closet floor straight	1	3	4	4			
0–4	Drawers and closet door closed	0	4	4	4			
0–4	Floor picked up	0	1	4	3			
0–4	Nightstand neat	0	4	4	4			
0–4	Desk top clean and neat	0	0	4	4			
0–4	Clothes neatly hung up	2	3	4	4			
0–10	Room dusted: dresser–2, book shelves–2, windowsills–2, desk–2, and baseboards–2	0	0	7	6			
0–4	Floor vacuumed	0	0	4	3			
		6	21	46	44			

5/16 Surprise Check — oops! Better luck next time!
5/17 Check at 11 A.M. sharp. Much better!
5/18 Check at 2 P.M. You made it! Great!
5/24 Check at 11 A.M. Super job — what a cleaner!

written on the form, giving several days' notice. Sue found that the children's examination of the master bedroom meant a white-glove type inspection and she had to labor diligently to pass. Treats were given for scoring from forty up to the possible fifty points. These prizes were kept very simple: a candy bar, an old motor found at a garage sale for the eleven-year-old to disassemble, or a special book from the library. She wanted the biggest reward to come from meeting the standard set on the inspection sheet, not from the token prize. Make this inspection sheet work for you. If toys and a toy shelf are the problem, add them to the sheet. Change the categories to fit the particular room you will be inspecting. If there are fifteen books sitting around on the nightstand, a limit of three books could be set. Adjust the inspection sheet to meet the situation in your home.

Children have different levels of motivation for keeping a room clean. We would hope that when they have their own homes, the inner motivation will increase because it is *theirs*. For now, you can help them organize their bedrooms and succeed in keeping them clean. If it comes to a clash, remember, the child's membership in your family is more important than a clean bedroom. If you can, give them the skills of housekeeping now, so that when or if they want to, they can employ them. If they won't accept this responsibility now, perhaps they will be ready to do so later. Two-year-old little Sarah was taught to say, "I can handle anything, I can handle anything." Such an attitude in life gives enough courage to say, "I will give it another try."

10: Managing Money

Your child's future happiness depends more on *how* he or she manages money than on *how much* they have. In order to manage money, they must have some money to manage. Since there are many valuable experiences to learn before the child is old enough to earn money outside the home, how will you provide some money to practice on? An allowance? Paid jobs? Or a little of both? You need to make this decision. Then, when the child has money, there are four parts to managing it: budgeting, saving, earning, and giving.

HOW WILL THEY GET MONEY?

The allowance system, especially in the early years, seems to be successful. Choosing to pay your child for every little job is a hassle, and the end result will likely be that they will no longer work when they no longer need money from Mom and Dad. Being paid for making the bed and picking up toys introduces a faulty premise because in the big world we generally do housekeeping without pay. Try to keep bedroom and regular household responsibilities as part of family membership rather than relating them to money. An allowance, perhaps so much per week or month for each year of age, would give enough money to experiment with for needs and wants. (Twenty-five cents per year of age for a seven-year-old would be $1.75.) That small amount certainly will not be all they need, but in the beginning it gives them enough to learn the value of various coins, how to make purchases, and then how to evaluate them. For instance, your young child may decide to buy a little gadget that will break in a day. You might offer advice, but do not impose your opinion by force. The reason for having some money to spend is so the child can learn the consequences of making choices. When the flimsy little toy breaks, don't say, "I told you so," but help the child evaluate why and consider possible alternative purchases next time.

One of the advantages to an allowance is that the child can count on it regularly, and practice budgeting and planning—two important lessons. Keeping allowances small enough so that they don't meet all growing wants as children enter teen years provides an incentive to earn more. Decision time: Will you provide the paying jobs, or will they earn money outside the home? It depends on your circumstances and the child's age. After about age twelve there can be opportunities to sell goods and services outside the family—things like caring for the neighbor's yard or pets during vacations, baby-sitting, or delivering a paper route. The challenge for parents is to carefully structure teaching situations that prepare their children for these working opportunities. Encourage them to take advantage of local training sessions, such as classes on baby-sitting, first aid, and proper care of equipment, like the lawn mower or bicycle. On the other hand, you could make opportunities to earn money at home, especially for work you might normally pay someone else to do, but this is in addition to their regular family duties. Then if they decide not to do it, you just hire someone else. Earning can be paid either by the job ($1.00 for stacking the wood), or so much for every half-hour labor. (Paying by the job gives incentive to get it done quickly and parents will not fret as much about getting their money's worth.) When Krista saw her mom deal out $3.50 an hour to a cleaning lady, she asked if she could do the cleaning because she needed gas money. These wise parents had not satisfied her total money wants, thus creating motivation. Working mothers earning a second income often make such a bargain with their children to baby-sit or do the things they find hard to do because of working.

BUDGETING

Teach children to manage money. They need many varied experiences throughout their growing years to learn planning, evaluating, and decision making. Give them experience in planning their own spending and help them understand the family budget. Most kids just spend until the money is gone, then wait until next pay day. It will be a great asset to them, and they will get more of what they really want, if they learn to set goals, plan, keep track of expenses, and re-evaluate their money habits.

Give the young child opportunities to buy. If she has selected a dot-to-dot book to purchase with her own money, let her count out the coins, hand the clerk the money, get some change back, and carry the paper sack. Schools offer many opportunities to practice money responsibility. When they carry the currency for school lunch, a field trip, or to buy a book, they are learning. There will be a few times that they lose their money. Help them find ways to carry it safely. Grandma used to tie coins in a cloth hankie or sew them in a lining. A zippered bag or sealed envelope with the child's name and what it is for help prevent loss as the child skips, tumbles, and runs to school.

To teach a child to manage money, you can create learning experiences. A good time to do this is with clothing purchases. Suppose it is August and you have sixty dollars to spend on filling in the empty spots of a wardrobe for your daughter. This is not much money for clothes these days, but if the planning and buying are done together by the parent and child, the child is likely to be more satisfied with the clothing selections and apply this experience when buying other things. She may take better care of the clothing and perhaps she will understand that trade offs have to be made when there is not enough money to buy everything new or buy it now. Sit down with the child with paper and pencil in hand. Write down the goal. What would she like? What does she already have? Are there things she could buy to complete or slightly change some outfits? You are teaching this girl to use logic, rather than to just buy what she sees and likes (impulse). Then you will talk about the money limit. There will be some cutbacks, postponements, and trade offs. Since this is the season of many sales, you can watch the papers, and then shop together. You can help her evaluate the fit, quality of material, and workmanship: "Is this what we want? Will it last?"

Budgeting opportunities can be structured to gradually give more and more responsibility to the child. One father gave his sixteen-year-old daughter $120 for a new coat. "I think you are old enough to make a good choice; you may shop and make this decision. But before you go, will you show me a list of your expectations? Promise me you will check this list before you buy, to answer the questions of whether you have picked the coat because it is what you really want, or you were attracted to it for the moment." This was her list:

MY MONEY

MARCH
month

Things I need	Things I want	Estimated plan for this month	
1. lunch	1. alarm clock	lunches	8.00
2. tennis shoes	2. dragon kite	shoes	17.00
3. deo	3.	deo	1.50
4.	4.	kite	7.00
5.	5.		
6.	6.		
			$33.50

These are my purchases

Item	Want	Need	Cost
lunch 3/4		✔	1.00
lunch 3/6		✔	1.00
movie 3/7	✔		3.00
shoes 3/10			16.86
birthday gift 3/10			5.13

1. I want this coat to be dressy enough for church and nice parties.
2. Warm enough for cold winter.
3. A moderate style to last three years.
4. Not to look like my mother's coat.

Sure enough, when she and her friend went shopping, she was first attracted to a shiny purple down parka. But she already had a ski jacket and continued looking because of her promise to Dad. She settled on a midi-length gray wool coat with delicate tucks, self-belt, and hood. She and her dad were both pleased.

Gradually give children more financial responsibility, preparing them for the time when they leave home and money management is totally theirs. One family has progressed to the point where they feel confident in giving each teen all his or her clothing and shoe allotment, school lunch money, bus fare, and allowance in one lump sum each month so the child can do his or her own budgeting. They write down their basic budget and then keep track of their purchases. Once in a while the kids make an unwise decision, or give in to an impulsive whim. What about loans? When you give the child a loan, let him pay it back. You may not need the money, but the child needs to learn to pay back obligations. If your child misuses money too often, back up a little. The simple chart that follows helps them see what they got for the money and whether or not they would spend it that way again.

Have your children keep an "I Want" list on which to write down those burning desires for things. When they get a little money, talk about what they really want most. They can *plan* their buying rather than spending by impulsive desire. It's unhealthy for the child to get everything he wants—most of us can't afford it anyway. Guide your child into purchases he can feel good about for a long time. Remember that saying: "Most unhappiness in the world is caused by giving up what you want most for what you want at the moment."

Another short-term lesson in budgeting might be to plan

your family vacation together, discussing the total money allotted, how much will be needed for gas, food and lodging, and how much will be left for fun and entertainment. As you plan the family budget, help the child plan a personal vacation budget for mementoes, T-shirt, and so forth. It can save on hundreds of requests ("Can I have this?"). You will not want to try all of these experiences at once, but one here and one there will eventually add up.

Involve your children in family budgeting and goal setting. When you set up and evaluate your spending plan, let your children express their desires and feelings. Give them experience. Josh learned how expensive food was by meal planning, list making, and shopping. After that he was more careful about opening the refrigerator to his friends. Don and Jane used a visual experience to help their children understand the family budget. Don turned in his paycheck for cash, brought it home and called everyone for a family-council meeting. The kids' eyes widened as they saw that much real money, but were disappointed as it went into each envelope for bills. They talked about getting a few of those dollars back by being more careful to close the outside doors, turn out lights, and maintain what they already had. Another family tried to create the same type of experience by using Monopoly money. Understanding the family financial plan, and seeing it discussed openly, will help children be able to choose a plan and handle their own affairs when they are adults. Older teens could also take a turn at balancing the family accounts and writing checks, although parents would have to sign them. You will probably need to mention that financial information is private and shared only within the family.

SAVING

Saving, a skill that goes along with money, must be done in little steps. You don't start by trying to get a child to put everything received into the bank for college. The child doesn't even know what college is yet, although Mom and Dad may have started an account for just that purpose. The child needs to learn to save with a goal in mind—something wanted—within reach of a week or two. Later, the child is capable of saving a little longer for something.

Sometimes it works to match the savings effort (dollar for dollar) for such an item as a bicycle. This will help the child adjust to realistic expectations—perhaps settling for a bike with fewer extras in order to have it sooner. Having to earn part of the cost frequently means better care and maintenance of the item, while it helps the child to get things otherwise beyond his or her financial abilities.

To make time for Bonnie to meet a publishing deadline, her children signed contracts to do paying jobs she normally would have done. Eight-year-old Becky worked with great fervor every day after school. Her goal: to buy windows for her playhouse. She set aside part of her earnings for the windows and another part for immediate spending—for books from the school book club or whatever. Some parents start their children, when they are very young, saving a specific percent of their money for "permanent savings," another part for "short-term savings" such as the playhouse windows, and the rest for "immediate desires." If you don't start a permanent savings program in the beginning, think about when you would rather help your children start one.

In a recent survey conducted by the *Denver Post,* of ninety-six eighth grade students, only *one* said she was saving money for college. Besides taking self-sustaining skills with them as your children leave your home, it will also boost their confidence to have some money—for tuition toward college or trade school, or to put down for a home or a business. One girl saved a thousand dollars from baby-sitting through her teen years. Later, as she approached marriage, she often reflected on the special purchases she could make. It was such a feeling of freedom. "Shall I buy dinnerware or cookware? Shall I save it to buy baby furniture for the child we hope to have some day? If I wanted to, I could spend it on. . . ." A couple of thou-

sand dollars could be wonderful. The student who pays for part of his higher-education tuition is more likely to take it seriously. Helping them save a little now for the future makes the habit easier as adults, and grown-ups find it nice to have a little money working for them also.

By the time a child is earning some of his own money, guide him into saving part of it. One midwestern family had this policy: "Either put twenty-five percent of your money into savings or pay twenty-five percent to Mom and Dad for room and board. In another family, two boys have paper routes. After their weekly collections, they dump the money in the middle of the floor (fun visual experience). First they take out enough to pay the paper bill, then a tithe for church. They talk about how much they will need for spending that week, considering birthdays or special activities that are scheduled. The rest goes directly to savings. This provides fantastic training as these boys go through this exercise every week. Though the parents are guiding, the boys still experience free agency. Remember: There is such a thing as a child having too much spending money. If children have money and are totally free to spend it with no obligations, they are learning a false supposition that may cause problems in adult life. You are not doing a child a favor by allowing complete, unguided spending. As adults, we have bills to pay—our money isn't just for fun, although we should each have a personal allowance with no strings attached.

When twelve-year-old Wesley got his first paying job, earning forty dollars a week, Bonnie went to the bank with him where he opened an account so he could cash his paycheck, deposit the agreed percent for savings, and walk away with the green that was his to spend. Before you have the money, it seems like it will buy much more than when you are actually laying it out. When the money is gone, with other things still to buy, there is a temptation not to save "this time." Depositing the savings money first was the solution for Wes. Children can be made aware that many employers have systems to withhold savings from the paycheck—helping them meet a goal of "savings first."

Where does the child keep money at home? Piggy bank, box, can, envelope, jar, or pile? A glass or clear plastic container has a very visual appeal, and one that can be easily opened is fun because the money can be taken out and counted. (One boy even liked to iron the bills.) As soon as the child is saving for a purchase, help him make a distinction between immediate spending money and short-term savings. Perhaps money for spending could be put in his wallet and money for savings in a bottle. Another way would be to have two zipper bags, one marked "spending money," the other marked for a goal like "bicycle fund." One caution: Advise the child not to keep too much cash at home and to put it away where others can't see it. It is tempting to neighborhood children, younger brothers and sisters or even thieves. (The top drawer in a bedroom chest of drawers is one of the first places a robber looks.)

EARNING AND GIVING

It takes a little maturity to be able to wait a week or two for the paycheck. When young children first start to work for pay, they need immediate payoffs: Sweep the porch now and receive a dime now. When a child has a desire to earn, create a way. One mother, whose children loved to go to garage sales, found that if the child earned the fifty cents, he was more careful in his choices. One time a nine-year-old swept the whole driveway (a hundred feet) and porches to earn fifty cents. He bought a record player that worked. Another mother went to the bank at the beginning of August and got twenty dollars' worth of coins and offered certain paying jobs (of course, after their regular chores and rooms were finished first) to earn money for school supplies. Their mother may have bought the supplies anyway, but this opportunity banished the August doldrums, taught lessons about the value of money, and motivated the students to take better care of their school things. (The coins were collected in a relish caddy that had three plastic bowls on which they taped their names, and it was kept on a kitchen shelf.) Just before school started, they made two lists—one list of wants and another of needs. They compared prices from the newspaper ads and went shopping. It was the highlight of the month, and the mother said she actually put out less on school supplies than in previous years.

Watch magazines, books, boutique, and craft sales for items your children can make to give or sell. When you give something as a gift that you have made, it carries with it pride and a feeling of accomplishment. When something you have made is good enough to sell it boosts the ego. In the third grade Bonnie made her spending money by weaving pot holders and paying her brother a commission for selling them. Nowadays, selling door to door is not always such a good idea, but local clubs, schools, or churches sometimes take things on consignment at their sales. Bobette likes to make "rice mice" to sell (little fabric mice filled with rice). Melea makes soft-sculpture faces out of nylons for tree ornaments. Hoping for great sales, Mattie (in kindergarten) made bells out of paper cups by covering them with aluminum foil. Bonnie talked Mattie into putting these bells up as decorations in their home, but she also helped him glue fuzzy fur on pencils to make "frustration pencils" for the school craft sale. Earning some of their own money gives children a "financial identity."

The story of all time happened in 1979 when eleven-year-old Wesley wanted to earn some Christmas money. His sisters had money from baby-sitting, which he wasn't old enough to do, and his parents wouldn't let him take on a paper route. Finally, Bonnie suggested he could take a *few* orders for homemade bread from the teachers at his elementary school. (Bonnie had been sending bread to bake sales and as gifts to the children's teachers for many years.) She taught Wes how to make bread (they have a mixer with a bread hook for kneading), and he took a sample loaf and a sign-up sheet to school and left it in the faculty lounge. (Naturally, he got permission from the principal first.) The first day, he had orders for fifty-nine loaves of rye bread (That's ten batches!). Every afternoon he made two batches of rye bread (twelve loaves), but he kept coming home with more and more orders. He was so caught up in his success and the fun that he had a hard time hearing mother say, "No more!" Wesley made a deal with his older sister to wash dishes for a share of the profits. In the end, he made about eighty loaves of bread, having only one batch fail. After paying for the ingredients, he had enough money to buy Christmas gifts for his younger brother, three sisters, Mom, Dad, and enough left for a digital watch. His enterprise hit the front page of the local newspaper—he loved the fame. In 1980 he decided on a different project, but Bonnie taught the other children who wanted to earn Christmas money to make bread, setting a limit of twelve loaves each.

With earning, teach your children the joy of giving. Being able to give, to give willingly, and in the right amounts are attitudes most parents will want to foster by creating opportunities for such experiences. At holiday time, try getting your own projects finished early so you can have time to help a child plan for, and make, or earn money and buy, gifts. Don't just buy a package of hankies for your daughter to give Dad on his birthday. There is so much fun in choosing and buying that you should involve the child in this part too, even if she can't keep a secret.

One couple who yearly gave ten dollars to a children's hospital decided to give their three young children the growing opportunity to earn and give. They set three baby food jars, each with a child's name on it, on the kitchen counter, and found ways for their little children to earn five of the ten dollars in "love pennies" for the sick children at the hospital. The children were paid immediately, or at the end of each day, for their little extra jobs. They loved seeing the pennies stack up, and counted them often. They really felt a part of buying crutches and medicine. Little children naturally have a loving and generous heart, and that attitude can be nurtured.

CAN I BABY-SIT TONIGHT?

If you decide to allow your children to baby-sit, help them to understand the responsibility involved. Help them to be prepared. Churches, schools, and community centers offer classes to teach child-care techniques, etiquette, and ways to entertain children. If such a class isn't available, check out a book at the local library. One child-care class suggests the baby-sitter make up a box, suitcase, or bucket in which to keep little things to entertain the children: little craft projects, games, a puppet or two, fingerplays, and some books to read. Laura is a highly sought-after baby-sitter. She doesn't just plop herself down in front of the television; she talks to the kids, and plays *with* them. Just before she leaves her home, she picks up some little project, record, or game to take with her from her own home that the children haven't seen before. Some young people, like Laura, have a natural, built-in instinct, but others can learn if the desire is there. Parents can assist in this job preparation.

One more suggestion. For your child's baby-sitting kit, include a tablet, or run off several forms like the following, for the baby-sitter to hand to the parents, to be quickly filled out before they depart for the evening. There is no need to be bashful. As an employee, your child needs to know these details in order to do a good job.

LAURA'S BABY-SITTING SERVICE

We will be at: _____

Phone: _____

We expect to be home at: _____
                                                time

Bed times: _____
                    child one

_____
      child two

_____
      child three

Neighbor's name and number in case of emergency:

_____
            name

_____
      phone number

Any other specific instructions: _____

_____

_____

My fee is $1.00 an hour and $1.50 an hour after midnight.

Laura

CAN I HAVE A PAPER ROUTE?

"Yes, but it is all yours. I don't have time to mess with it," is an often-heard answer. When you want your children to learn to read, do you just put a book down in front of them? No. You send them to school. There aren't many teachers for paper routes, but the parent can be the tutor for marketing and collection techniques. Dean, who was twelve, folded the papers and delivered them willingly every day, but he hated collecting. The district advisor said, "If he doesn't collect, he loses the job," a natural consequence. Quitting now would be teaching him to fail, and if he has a problem, he's only learning to run away from it. The parents decided to help him succeed for several months, to learn the lessons every creditor knows. These parents considered the time helping him an investment in his future career. They found the reason Dean hated to collect was that he was intimidated by a few rude people. No one keeps a tally, but if a record were kept, you would see the grouch has actually been rewarded for being harsh because he can get by without paying fifty percent of the time. Dean's parents practiced with him at home, pretending to be the grouch at the door. Sometimes they went with him. They were teaching Dean to be assertive, to stand up for his own rights, but to still be polite—valuable adult skills.

Eric Monson's parents helped him organize his deliveries by making a map showing every house in his district. They drove the route and plotted out each house. They blackened boxes to indicate customers who took daily papers; red showed Sunday only, and clear stood for houses where he didn't deliver. It was easy for a substitute to make deliveries with his plan. The original map was slipped in a protective plastic envelope. For ten cents a month Eric could make a copy and cross off homes that had paid, for a quick visual picture of those who still owed.

Marketing techniques are important. Eric found that the first month he had his route, he collected thirteen dollars more in tips than the last carrier just because he porched the papers.

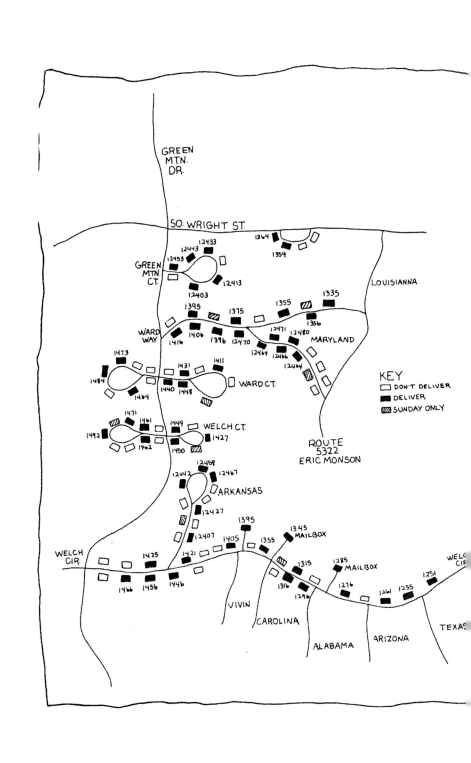

For one dollar he sent away for gummed labels to stick on his receipts that read "Eric Monson, *Post* Paper Boy" with his phone number—a little professional touch that saved him from finger cramps filling in all the receipts. He pays a friend one dollar an hour to go with him collecting—a witness is sometimes helpful and a friend makes it safer and more fun. (His paper company offers theft insurance for just twenty-five cents a month).

Jamie's dad, who is a salesman himself, helped his son write an introductory letter when he started his route. "When people know you, they care more about you." It started like this: "Hello. I am Jamie and I am nine years old. I have four sisters and three brothers. I am glad to serve you. Please call me if there is any problem. The reason I have taken this route is. . . ." Now when this sharp boy, with his dark hair and eyes and ready smile, stops at a door, they know him. The next principle his dad taught; "Tell them you are coming." When it is time to collect, Jamie slips a notice in with the paper, "I will be by tonight between 6:30 and 8:00 to collect $5.50 due for August's *Rocky Mountain News.*" This idea helped overcome some of the "I don't have change tonight" excuses. After he has tried to collect twice and no one has been home, he leaves an addressed envelope and a nice request asking them to mail it to him. Adults who deliver large routes with hundreds of papers often just slip an envelope in with the paper at the end of the month and expect the payment to be mailed just like any other bill.

It is good to have a job where regular, consistent performance is required. Baseball, swimming, and other extracurricular activities develop skills and discipline, but they don't teach personal responsibility in the same way that a job does. Kids need to learn to succeed at work.

11: Evaluating

"Why didn't it work? My children are not doing their chores. Their bedrooms are messy." Take the time *now* to reflect, before you plan your next strategy. Maybe you have asked too much and it is beyond the child's mental or physical capabilities. Perhaps the child didn't understand the assignment and needs retraining. There could be something wrong with the parental approach or techniques. Sometimes incentives, rewards or consequences need to be initiated to motivate performance.

The problem can be with the task, the physical arrangement, the child, or the parent. Take a careful look. Analyze the situation. Brainstorm possible solutions—it may help to write them down so you can make a rational decision. Then make a new plan. The very reason this book was written is to give you many ideas from which to choose or to trigger your own imagination for techniques to approach the work from a new angle. Most of parenting is on-the-job training. We learn as we go. How we respond after the child's first efforts to do a job can be the key as to whether they will try again, procrastinate, slip by with a halfway-done job, or quit. Let us go through a series of self-examining questions to clarify the causes and symptoms of such problems, so you can go back and rework the training program.

Are the standards clear? Sally, age twelve, likes to know exactly what is expected. Does cleaning the bathroom include only sweeping the floor, or mopping it, too? When Dad checks to see if the bathroom is clean, Sally wants to say, "Yes, I did everything required, even sweeping the floor." Set a clear standard by posting a cleaning specification card listing the daily and weekly requirements for a particular room or job, giving the child the opportunity to compare her work to the standard, even if Mother and Dad are not at home. Specific examples of the job cards are on page 59.

The child needs to plainly understand
1. The rule or your expectations of the job.
2. The positive advantages and the consequences if it is not done.
3. The option he or she has to choose between the reward or consequence.
4. Exactly which choice the parent prefers the child to make.

Does the child understand your vision of a finished job? We adults use the closure principle of our advantage when we evaluate our children's work. Let us explain. Can you read "Cl__n__ng c__n b__ m__r__ f__n __f y__ __ h__v__ t__m__ __ff r__g__l__rl__?" After a few seconds, most people read it easily as "Cleaning can be more fun if you have time off regularly." We fill in the missing vowels because we are very familiar with word patterns. When our children work on a job, their understanding and experience are different from ours. Have you taught every part of the job? One twelve-year-old boy, when sent to wash the car, just squirted cold water over the car and expected it to be clean. He hadn't paid attention to his dad using a sponge, bucket, and sudsy water. He had to be taught those steps. It is easy to assume that our children know skills they do not know because we are so familiar with them. Watch for untaught details. Another problem with the closure principle is that parents fill in gaps or reach conclusions without fully listening to the child. Ask questions and be sure you understand what the child is trying to express.

Can the child handle the job? If the child cannot handle the job you want done, there are three options:

1. Make it easier or lower the standards.
2. Change the job entirely.
3. Provide review and practice.

The trick is to evaluate your retraining approach objectively, free from emotion—specifically from anger or frustration.

If you can sense that the child simply cannot handle the job, don't hesitate to change it. Dwight, age six, wanted to water the house plants, and mother decided to let him try. She carefully marked the watering days on a chart and showed him how much water to give each plant. However, Dwight consistently got carried away when dumping on the water. He needed time to mature before handling this responsibility. To compromise, Mother gave him an opportunity to be the "Official Patio Squirter." Watering down or washing off the patio with the hose once a week was enjoyable enough that he willingly turned the plant watering back to his mother.

In order for a child to change his or her behavior, it may sometimes be necessary to change the parent's behavior. A horse trainer can break a horse successfully, send it back to its owner, and in three weeks all the training can be undone. The owner has to be broken of the wrong signals he is giving the horse. Children also sense our expectations and know whether we mean what we say. If we think through our requests, making them reasonable and fair, and then follow through with consequences, we are more likely to be taken seriously.

In the "Ugly Duckling" story, the mother duck does not want to accept the swan as one of her ducklings; he looks different, sounds horrid, and is big and awkward. In one recorded version of this story, the mother duck watches as the ugly duckling swims and then she squawks, "He swims very well; he must be mine!" It is easy to be loving and accepting, when our children swim well; it's more difficult when they flounder. Evaluate the causes for their floundering, replan, and try again.

Are you taking time for inspections?   Checking up on a job after the child says it is done doesn't mean you do not trust the child; rather that you value the assignment and the efforts enough to carry through to the end.

- Taking time to inspect provides an opportunity to give verbal rewards, positive strokes.
- Taking time to inspect gives you an opportunity to foster thorough work habits.
- Taking time to inspect can break the self-defeating cycle of procrastination.

This does not mean you inspect every job that the child ever does. After the job has been completed properly several times, a simple question about the completion of the job gives a chance to build integrity. The child says "I did the job!" and you accept the answer. When inspecting your child's work, these suggestions might be helpful:

1. Avoid damaging the atmosphere over "nothing." The bulky wrinkle in John's bed should be overlooked if John's friends are waiting at the door and he has already spent half an hour picking up and straightening.
2. Postpone inspecting when your fuse is short. Parents in a rotten mood tend to be overly critical and quick to find fault.
3. Give the child time off. When a job is poorly done, sometimes a break before correcting it can ease tension. Even when a job is not finished, the child may need time off. School is work for children, and they need some time to unwind after their "jobs."
4. Evaluate the child's performance on the basis of the room's condition before the job was started, rather than on what has not been done. If the living room had been cluttered with papers, toys, and books, consider that those items have all been put away, not that the sofa pillows are askew.
5. Shun words like always, never, and every time. Also avoid references to past mistakes: "You always forget to make your bed!" or "You never hang up your coat!" Rather, concentrate on and discuss only the present assignment.

Are you exercising too much control? If so, the child wants to be told what to do next, or to be told what he is not doing that he should be doing. In Berlin, Germany, a kindergarten teacher whose class was made up half of German and half of American students, observed that the German children took longer to develop inner controls than the American children in her somewhat loosely structured classroom. She felt this was due to the strong, strict structure in most German homes compared to the more relaxed, less authoritarian style of American families.

Shauna was disappointed that her seven-year-old son was such a dawdler. For him, putting on socks was a twenty-minute task. Shauna was constantly after him: "Hurry, you'll be late. Put on your shirt now and then your jeans." "Don't forget to make your bed." "Come on, it's time to eat." Lynn's bedroom had two doors; one opened onto the kitchen, making his every action visible to his mother as she prepared breakfast, and she took advantage of this by giving directions to his every move. At a parent conference, Lynn's teacher reported, that he needed to take more responsibility for completing his schoolwork on time. That triggered the idea for rearranging Lynn's room to build more responsibility at home as well. The kitchen door was closed off by moving furniture in front of it. Since Lynn did not want to miss breakfast or be late for school and the responsibility had been placed on his shoulders, he managed to get ready on time without his mother's constant vigil. Let the child make as many of his own choices as possible and handle his own responsibilities.

Does the child see disorder? How can we train children to be responsible for their own things, to notice a book dropped on the floor and put it back on the shelf? One frustrated mother set a kitchen chair right in the middle of the doorway to her daughter's bedroom. She thought to herself, "I bet my daughter and her friend, Tammy, who is spending the night, will never even think to move it." Sure enough, they played, ate dinner, got dressed for bed, popped popcorn, and listened to records, were in and out of that room all night, and never once thought to move the chair in the doorway, not even to set it aside. They climbed over or squeezed around it all night. Because seeing dirt and clutter is a skill that usually has to be learned, just like tying a shoe, it requires training, practice, and retraining.

Is the child balking? Robert L. DeBruyn suggests there are three roadblocks to teaching a child: the alibis, the objections, and the complaints. It may help to understand these roadblocks before you decide which retraining option to use: lowering the standard, changing the job, or giving more practice.

The child who offers an alibi or an excuse might say, "I didn't have time to make my bed" or "I will clean the bathroom tomorrow." If the neglected job must be done, you can respond rapidly by saying, "We'll wait on breakfast while you make your bed" or "You can clean the bathroom during the TV time tonight." A child who uses alibis regularly is showing a lack of interest and needs your understanding, if you want her to gain that interest back. Try to react calmly, but with an immediate solution, and then make time later for open communication about the real cause behind the alibi giving. Does your child feel that her load is too heavy? Are there unusual pressures at school? Would a more responsible job give more interest and meaning?

Children can feel tremendous pressures from schoolwork, teachers, peers, and coaches. Sue's daughter remembers a science teacher who resented the extra time required for band projects. He wanted her to give everything to his science class, and deliberately assigned heavy homework to coincide with music festivals and concerts. Pulling rank like this at home will only lead to poor family relationships. Try to understand the causes of the alibi. The best option will likely be altering or changing the assigned jobs, rather than holding to a dead-end course.

The child who makes excuses or objects to assigned tasks is generally looking for more attention from the parent, more help with the job, or more time to complete it. "But I can't do this, it's too hard." "But I have to practice piano now." "But Tom was coming over. I can't help!" The objection may be valid. Listen carefully and then make adjustments accordingly. It is easy to let excuses turn into arguments, so avoid this by asking your child to explain the objection more carefully. If the excuse indicates strong emotion, reassure the child gently.

Give credit for the thought, and compliment the child on the good points (there surely will be one or two), and then insist that the job be done as assigned.

The "broken record" technique can be employed with children when they object to doing their work. How long can you listen to a scratched record that sings repeatedly, "love will, love will, love will, love will, love will"? The impulse is to immediately move the needle over and hear the rest of the song. You can use the broken-record technique with your children. Camille had put off doing the dishes all day, instead she munched on goodies, talked to her teen friends on the phone, and read a favorite book. At 4 P.M. her mother knew the kitchen clutter had to be cleaned up so dinner preparations could begin at five. She said, "Camille, do the dishes now." Camille responded with an excuse and a "Who, me!" look. Mother calmly replayed the statement, "Camille, do the dishes now." After several more repetitions, Camille decided to do the dishes rather than continually hear the request, thus stopping the broken record. Effective use of this requires a calm, unemotional command on the parent's part, with a simple, direct statement of what must be done. Once the needle has been jarred, give encouragement as the job progresses and praise when the job is completed. Use this technique when a situation can no longer be let go and must be confronted. The broken record is not the same as nagging. Nagging involves finding fault by constant scolding and can last many hours or even days! The broken record asks for immediate action. Once the action is under way, take the record off and change the tune to praise and encouragement.

Complaining children can be the most annoying. Is it because a valid complaint threatens the parent's ego? "I have to do more work than any of my friends." "Why can't Mary do this instead of me? It isn't fair!" Children who complain are usually upset, but not always upset about what they are complaining of. Michelle can complain about washing the dishes but really be upset about a poor grade on a history test. Hearing the child out can do a lot to clear the air or the foggy complaint. Napoleon supposedly said, "When people cease to complain, they cease to think." If the complaint is supported by fact, make corrections right away and don't be afraid to admit that you were wrong.

Even as adults we use alibis, objections, and complaints to procrastinate doing an unpleasant job. Your children will be served well by learning to understand the reasons they give for not doing an assigned job.

Does your child procrastinate? Some procrastination seems to be normal in all of us. The trick is to stop procrastination from becoming a habit. To do this, learn to recognize the symptoms, possible reasons, and then focus on some suggested solutions to stop the procrastination tendency.

The procrastinating child sometimes
 • Puts off starting a job or assignment
 • Is slow in doing or finishing anything
 • Does messy or incomplete work
 • Is overly careful and meticulous
 • Waits for help
 • Gives many excuses
 • Seldom notices things that need doing
 • Displays lack of interest
 • Stays away from home to avoid assignments

Possible reasons for procrastinating
 • Discouraged because the work is too difficult
 • Parents expect perfection
 • Fear of failure
 • Experiences too many failures and too few successes
 • May be bored because the work is too easy
 • Not having to do it last time may have paid off
 • Health or physical deficiencies
 • Cover-up for lack of know-how
 • Watches too much television

- Parents' requests may be inconsistent: two hours today and none tomorrow

Solutions to try
- Praise the child for positive efforts
- Help the child develop skills through which success can be felt
- Set up regular assignments with chore charts
- Give the child something special to do
- Find out whether there are physical or health problems
- Adjust work to the child's level
- Be near to see that the child starts work promptly
- Insist that the child stay at the job until it is finished
- Time assignments and have the child try to beat the record.
- Offer fun incentives from time to time

Is there a set time to work? Is the schedule different every day? Is the child expected to do some work today and none tomorrow? A simple schedule with regular eating times and bed times helps children regulate their lives. Are the assignments made ahead of time or are they issued at the last minute? Is this child treated as a valuable employee rather than a slave? Are you expecting too much? Is there a problem with the job? Is it too hard? Is it so big or will it take so long that it overwhelms the child? No one is perfect; we cannot expect it of our children either. Are you treating your child with the same understanding you would give a neighbor's child? Remember that on the average kids keep their rooms cleaner than parents keep the garage.

Is there outside competition from friends, television, or books? Even though these can be good things, they need some regulation to keep life balanced. Your children will need time to work without playmates being around, and you will need some way to regulate it. At times it is children who do not belong to the family who are creating a problem, not only by their presence, but by their play habits. These children can find it enthralling to explore toys, closets, and drawers, pulling everything out and making a giant mess. In this case, it is necessary for the adult to guide these outsiders in playing within acceptable bounds. Arrange a pick-up time before the other children leave to help them realize the consequence of such curiosity. Adults also need to assume responsibility for a younger child's messes sometimes, to avoid building up resentment from the older children in the family.

Bonnie found it was her youngest child who caused most of the competition in their house at work time. He did everything imaginable to keep his older sisters and brother involved with him. When he was too young to help, Bonnie had him take a warm bath with plenty of tub toys to keep him occupied while the others worked. By the time he was four, the best solution was to put him to work, so he felt like he belonged.

Because watching television is a passive activity, it hinders work, slows learning, stifles creativity, and contributes to sibling aggressiveness. Yes, some knowledge can be gained from television viewing, but the child learns less in a passive way than if actively involved. Statistics indicate that children who watch television for four hours or more a day have lower I.Q.s than those who watch for less than four hours. Television interferes with work by making children less observant of their surroundings. They don't notice things that need to be done. When they try to work with the television on, it turns the iron in their blood to lead in their bottoms. When they lose interest in a show, they start picking at each other. Try turning the television off for several days. After the initial withdrawal symptoms, children begin to initiate activities for themselves and develop better interpersonal relationships. They become responsible for their entertainment instead of turning to the tube the instant they are bored. Most families don't choose to live without television, but they might make gains by cutting back.

Books, depending on the type, can do some of the same

things as television. After a dramatic reading, there is a let-down, an adjustment to the real world. Sometimes there is a short period of depression, which makes it hard to start back to work or attack homework. Reading can be a quick escape and means of procrastinating that makes it hard to pick up relationships again.

Is it a time of adjustment for the child? Have you read magazine articles before that say, "Dad and mom need a decompression time when they come home from work to acclimatize to the change in environment"? Children, as well as adults, have such adjustment needs. Watch for those needs after school or coming back from the other parent's homes, Grandma's, a slumber or birthday party. One mother said, "My children have trouble re-entering family life after Saturday morning cartoons are turned off." Another working mother found that if she gave her two-year-old a few minutes of her time right after she returned from work, by reading him a story or taking him for a walk, that the toddler would then play by himself while dinner was being prepared.

Maybe it is the need for such adjustment time that started the cookie-and-milk habit after school. One teen-age boy and his parents agreed on a hand signal to be used when stress was mounting—a kind of "let me adjust" sign. Parents who are aware can be understanding and monitor demands at volatile times.

Are you competing with an ex-spouse or other parents? Children whose parents are divorced often fantasize that the other parent wouldn't make them work or discipline them to the same degree. We don't have an answer to that problem, but it may help to know it exists. Even children who have two blood parents at home fantasize that other parents would treat them better. Do you ever think that someone else's kids would behave better than yours? Sometimes we even compete with an image of how parents a hundred years ago reared their children to be dutiful workers and good spellers too. The "olden days" probably were not all that wonderful.

Is it the parent who has a problem? Are *you* under stress? Are you expecting the child to carry your overload? If it can be avoided, don't try to discuss problems with a child when either of you is tired (after 10 P.M.), hungry (before mealtime), or ill. When the parent is under stress, it may be necessary to take an energy audit, assess the priority of goals, and postpone or drop some less important items. One mother, who had just recently taken an outside job, felt her family would be disappointed if they couldn't make fruitcakes and dip chocolates for the holidays as had been their tradition. When she asked them, she was surprised to learn they preferred to make carameled popcorn and party mix made from pretzels, cereal, and nuts. And these were much easier to make.

When the parents are experiencing stressful times, the children do not always react with increased help and mature understanding. We look back through time with rose-tinted glasses and draw the distorted conclusion that in old days families, including the children, all pulled together during hard times. We see a few exceptional experiences portrayed in the movies, but not all life is like that. Often, when parents go through a divorce, loss of a job, or severe illness, the children can't handle it. If this is the case, recognize it and get help. Look to your family, church, school, self-help groups, and professional counseling services.

The mother with a full-time, paying job sometimes has to cope with highly stressful circumstances. If the children are at a day-care center while she is at work, the house stays as is while they are gone, but when older children are at home on their own before and after school, some ground is lost. The working mother is generally a little more careful about keeping up with the necessities and not letting things pile up because of the rigid time structure and her limited hours at home. Statistics indicate the stay-at-home woman spends more time house cleaning than the woman with a paying job. One reason is that she takes on more projects. Whether the mother works outside the home or not, children grow by learning to help at home.

In the movie *Kramer vs. Kramer,* the morning after the mother walked out, the father and son are shown trying to fix breakfast together. If it had been the dad who had left the home, the mother would have fixed breakfast alone and set it on the table for the son to eat. When a woman takes a paying job or is burdened with extra stress and emotion, she has a tendency to still carry the traditional household duties too. A man thrown into the new circumstances of taking care of a home and children along with work tends to turn to the kids and to organize as a group. Since it is a period of new learning for him, he involves the children in the new adjustment, rather than protecting them from it, as a mother often does. Some women are afraid to let others take over part of the responsibility and give up some of the nurturing arts. Other women can't face the added stress of trying to teach the children new skills and figure it is easier to do it themselves.

If the working mother is willing to let others do part of the work, the principles and tricks that have been discussed for getting your children to work will be helpful. Many people have been successful at creating a "working family," rather than just working parents. You may be surprised at how much a child can do. When Beverly went to work full time, she turned most of the general cleaning and pick-up over to the children and she did one little deep-cleaning project each night to keep up. Some families divide the work, including cooking duties, into lists according to the number of family members, and rotate lists each week. This is successful when all the family members have relatively equal ability—perhaps all are over ten years of age. Mary Jane asks each child to give one full hour to house cleaning on Saturday, besides taking care of their own bedrooms. This is enough to keep their large home clean, and no one is burdened with working all weekend. Such cooperating families grow closer together and develop a healthy dependency upon each other.

With the second parent working, there is sometimes a little surplus money and the option is taken to hire someone else to do part of the cleaning. Some children conclude, "If we have to pay someone, I had better take extra care to keep it clean," while others take the "hotel" approach and relinquish all responsibility because "it's the maid's job." Other parents agree to pay their children rather than a housekeeper, giving the child responsibility and the opportunity to earn money.

For the working parent to get control at home, the trick is to faithfully keep up with the basics, pick-up, meals, dishes, and laundry, and gain the children's cooperation. An effort to incorporate the following may be helpful:

1. Tidy is the general rule. The level of housekeeping is relaxed, but clutter and filth are not acceptable.
2. Set up a program of maintenance to keep up what has been cleaned.
3. Make sure assignments are very explicit, telling who, what, when, and how.
4. Simplify housekeeping by making a place for everything, storing treasures and throwing out the unnecessary.

Are you angry? There are times when you have tried all 401 tricks and your kids still won't work. They feel they are doing all they should, and you feel they are skimping. You get upset and try using force. Then you try the "poor me" approach: "It takes fifty hours to cook and wash and clean this house and I can't do it all alone. Why can't you work for one hour?" The best thing to do is take a long walk and cool off. Re-evaluate the circumstances. It may be you, the parent, who has been so busy you aren't doing your share of the work and are trying to get the children to take over more than their share. In this case it might work to stay up until midnight doing the cleaning and try again tomorrow with a clean slate. All kinds of things can go wrong, and they will. The goal—to get the child to work—is right. Keep looking for a way to make it work. Remember, a clean house is not an end in itself. The whole reason for keeping house is the people: to make it easier to live, to be healthy, to improve self-images. Don't make the house the all-important thing and destroy the people in the process.

Are you intimidated by what others think or do? Have you fantasized that the Monsons' and McCulloughs' children pick up each thing they walk past, keep their rooms spotless, and do their chores without prompting? Part of the motivation to write this book was to find and experiment with solutions to overcome these problems. We hope others can benefit from what we have learned; however, our children try to slip by too, and procrastinate just like yours. Don't compare your children with what you think someone else's child is doing. Keep this whole business friendly. Don't expect your children to run faster than their strength. One night, at the end of a phone conversation, Bonnie's closing comment was "I have to go now and scrub the kitchen floor." "What do you mean," chided the caller. "Your kids should do that for you. I always scrubbed the floor for my mom." Get this, readers: OUTSIDERS OFTEN SEE YOUR CHILDREN AS UNTAPPED SOURCES OF LABOR, like an artesian well. Don't be intimidated. Bonnie explained to the caller that her children were currently enrolled in other housekeeping subjects at the present and they couldn't be expected to learn or do everything all in one semester. Often, when you have problems, others tend to advise, "Get your children to do more." Set your goals and follow your own course.

When trying to make changes, understand the family will fight change and it might get worse before it will get better. No pain, no gain. We each have a role we play in the family—just like an actor on stage. And when one member starts to change, even for the better, the other family members are subconsciously fearful it will disturb their roles or positions, so they fight the change, even sabotage it. Suppose Mom decides to be a better housekeeper. She reads *Bonnie's Household Organizer* book on home management and tries the ideas out at home.

Instead of the family reacting with increased support, they may sabotage her efforts until they realize this new change will not hurt their individual roles. The same thing happens when Dad goes on a diet. About the fifth day, Mom will get a tremendous urge to bake his favorite cherry pie, which she normally bakes once a year. You see, to instigate change, we must thoroughly know where we want to go and why, so these resistances to change won't set us back. There is a need for a good supervisor to stick to a goal, be patient, and keep trying to bring about a change.

As you judge the results of your efforts, consider that you are "improving" rather than in a final state of "improved." There is no such thing as a perfect parent—so why feel guilty if you aren't. That's the very reason so many parents don't like Mother's Day or Father's Day. They don't feel they fit the image. The child and parent both go through the growing seasons with ups and downs. If we accept ourselves as people who are trying and improving, we can more easily live with ourselves and continue trying.

After you have taught your children and they are old enough to be on their own, let go. You have tried to foster independence and teach responsibility whenever possible. Now is the time to continue to love them, but let go of other parts of their lives. One mother keeps telling her twenty-eight-year-old married daughter that she can't nickname her baby Lizzy. A father is insisting that his married son go to college. A seventy-six-year-old mother continues to tell her fifty-year-old daughter how she has to spend her money. Teach children to govern their own lives and then let go. There is still a place for friendship, but there are territories the children are responsible for themselves. If there are faults in their personalities, it is up to them to change. If they want skills, it is up to them to pay for and learn them. It is not necessary for parents to carry their adult children's financial and emotional responsibility the rest of their lives. However, families can be a great support system in helping over hard times. No one knows all the reasons why some children turn out to be champs and others turn out to be chumps. This book can't guarantee success, only improved chances.

In the years between now and the time your children leave home, set goals, continue looking for ways to make use of opportunities for them to work at home, have some fun, and reap the benefits. D. O. McKay said:

> The privilege to work is a gift,
> The power to work is a blessing,
> And the love of work is success.

12: 401 Ways to Get Your Child to Work at Home

Following are principles, methods, and tricks for getting children to work. The tricks are designed to keep it interesting and fun; they give extrinsic motivation until the child wants to do it for himself. The principles are included because if they are ignored the tricks won't work. Organization methods make work easier for children as well as adults. Using the right methods to teach a job help him do it—and that's what we are after. Use this gigantic list as a resource to brainstorm actions when you are looking for ideas. Reap the rewards of having measurable help at home, recognize the personal growth in your child's independence, and enjoy your extra time.

WORK MOTIVATORS

☐ Use paper plates for dinner and ask for volunteers to do the dishes.

☐ Have children play as if they are horses on a merry-go-round and pick up an item each time they go down and around.

☐ "Sneak up" on a job, when it looks hard by doing a little at a time.

☐ Wind up one another, and pretend to be "work robots."

☐ Play like a stiff-legged animal or a mechanical doll as you clean.

☐ Wind up a music box or musical animal and see how much of a room can be picked up before the music stops.

☐ Substitute song phrases like, "She'll be comin' round the mountain . . ." for "She'll (or He'll) be washing all the dishes, yes sireeee," or "She'll be setting out the silver, one, two, three."

☐ Plan a trip to Mars on a spaceship, gathering all the debris in the yard and bagging it for disposal in outer space.

☐ Have a leaf-raking party, serve "leaf chips" (potato chips) and dip for refreshment.

☐ Play Beat the Clock, as you do chores.

☐ Divide the family into work teams for companionship and conversation during work sessions.

☐ Try a twenty-item pick-up or five-minute pick-up with everyone helping.

☐ Change roles for an evening, letting the child act as the parent and the parent act as the child. Bedtime may be very different!

☐ Have a Green Thumb Party, to plant flowers or a garden. As refreshment serve green punch.

☐ Encourage children to send thank-you notes by providing them with their own note cards and stamps.

☐ Hand the child a dry plastic scrubber to get mud off shoes and boots.

☐ Sew a mit for kids to use while washing the car by sewing two sides of an old toilet seat cover or piece of a scatter rug together.

☐ Make a suggestion box that contains ideas, activities, and projects for kids to do when bored.

☐ Sing together like army troops do when they march. It makes a chore like leaf raking, snow shoveling, or weed pulling seem easier.

☐ Give stars for completed jobs. Have a little booklet stapled together for children to collect the stars in and have the full booklet redeemable for a Time with Parent.

☐ Let children draw pictures on sheets of paper with fabric crayons. Transfer these pictures to large pockets on an apron. As your children clean, let them wear the apron, placing items that belong to different family members in the appropriate pockets.

☐ Give children a glove, a small paint brush, or a feather duster, to make dusting possible in hard-to-reach places.

☐ Make a Dust Muppet from an odd sock. Use markers or liquid embroidery to paint on a face.

☐ Motivate the young child who is learning to read, by writing assignments in simple phrases like, "pick up toys," or "clean the sink."

☐ Use a special tablecloth chosen or designed by the child when it is the child's turn to cook.

- [ ] Make a Pick-up Puppet the child can use to pick up toys.

- [ ] Tack a sheet of paper on a wall or bulletin board for each child. Each time they put one of their toys away, they can draw a picture of that toy on their piece of paper. Use a special set of markers for this privilege.

- [ ] Draw names to be Helpful Elves to each other for a week, similar to the elves who helped the little old shoemaker.

- [ ] Pretend to be a traveling salesperson. Take a suitcase and pick up all items belonging to you, and take them to your "hotel room" to be put away.

- [ ] Play the game Putting Toys to Bed at bedtime.

- [ ] Have young children wear an apron for kitchen clean-up. Use trucks for picking up and hauling away, and carry a mail bag to deliver toys to their rightful places.

- [ ] Have the child put away ten items in a room and then have the parent try to guess what was put away. They love it!

- [ ] Give your wishes in an unusual way. Sing, "It would be so nice to have the living room vacuumed before 10 A.M." Sing it to a make-believe listener, but in earshot of the dawdling youngster.

- [ ] The parent can act as Toy Catcher, putting misplaced toys in the Toy Pound. To free the toy, the child must pay the fine by doing a special service for the parent.

- [ ] Record job assignments on a tape recorder, for after-school instructions. This is helpful when the parent can't be home, and is faster than writing them down.

- [ ] Let children help select seeds and flower or vegetable seedlings when you initiate their help with gardening.

- [ ] Change the words to "Here We Go Round the Mulberry Bush" to "This is the way we make our bed."

☐ Say to the child, "I am reminding you to sweep the stairs." If you pay a wage for jobs, then have a ten-cent charge for each time you remind your children to do a job. Record the time and date on a slip of paper and give it to the child on pay day.

☐ Assign someone to be the Sanitation Engineer, to collect trash around the house in a Litter Box or Litter Bag.

INCENTIVES

☐ Give incentives. They can be food, privileges, money, adult time, etc.

- Adult time: read a story, talk together, play a game, work a puzzle, make a project, or cook together.

- Privileges: play with a friend, roll out biscuits, have a lemonade stand, swim, ride a bike, paint, watch TV, or go roller skating.

- Food: red apple, cookie, banana, ice cream, peanuts, popsicle, sunflower seeds, soda pop, oyster crackers, box of animal cookies, dry cereal, or small candies.

- Things: small toy, game, record, money, cards, marbles, ball and jacks, crayons, colored pencils, ream of paper, tablet, book, clay, scissors, paints, top, jump rope, coloring book, gold fish, dress-up clothes, or rhythm toys.

☐ Proclaim the child royalty for the day on his birthday—no work!

☐ Create some "fun money," like dollar bills with blanks for name, job, and the amount of real money or privileges the job is worth.

☐ Award trophies made from paper, tin cans, papier-maché, or boxes. Announce categories ahead of time. They might include Neatest Trash Taker-Outer, Cleanest Bedroom, or Willing Go-for.

☐ Hide the family money set aside for Friday night entertainment in the family room. Have everyone work on cleaning the room to find it.

☐ Let children put old, heavy socks on their feet and skate around on a newly waxed floor to polish it. Be sure the floor is in good condition and smooth, so no one gets stuck with slivers.

☐ See that the child succeeds at something.

☐ Criticize the job, not the worker.

☐ Do not hang a mountain of work on every pending privilege.

☐ Put up a clothes line along a wall on which to hang school papers and art projects.

☐ Leave a note on your child's bed saying, "The Phantom made the bed!"

☐ Before discarding the child's art projects and drawings, take snapshots of them, to save a memory for the scrapbook.

☐ Send Happy Grams giving written acknowledgment of a job well done.

☐ Designate a special wall for Warm Fuzzies, or start your own Hall of Fame.

☐ Teach the child to use a Good Deed Sheet to record things done for family members.

☐ Buy some blue ribbon to make special family awards.

☐ Try the Undressing Game to teach children to take clothes off right side out (see page 110).

☐ Dress a "mop doll," to be hostess for a week in the cleanest bedroom.

☐ Talk a friend into being House Fairy to inspect your children's bedrooms. In exchange you might agree to inspect the bedrooms in your friend's house in a similar manner.

☐ Inventory your child's likes so you'll know natural interests and possible incentives.

☐ Give vigor to your positive compliments.

☐ Make your strokes specific rather than general.

☐ Keep a tally sheet of the positive strokes you give your child. Increase the number tomorrow.

☐ Draw a smiling face on your child's hand. Say, "Whenever you look at this, know it means I love you."

☐ Use immediate incentives for the young child.

☐ Write a love note twice a week.

☐ "Work before fun" gives incentive to get it done. Put something less desirable before something more desirable.

☐ Use popcorn as an incentive.

☐ Structure rewards, if possible, so that everyone has a chance to win.

☐ "Clean up before eating" might be an incentive for washing up a food-preparation mess.

☐ Keep a supply of balloons in reserve for rewards.

☐ Start an ice-cream club for achievements.

☐ Give out chances for good behavior or helpfulness. Later these can be drawn from a box for a prize.

☐ Work during television commercials.

☐ Cut out a line of connected paper dolls and write a "warm fuzzy" statement on each doll for your child.

☐ Use exciting job titles: The Filing Clerk clips and organizes coupons from magazines and newspapers. The Handyperson makes simple household repairs. The Storage Clerk puts groceries away and straightens cupboards.

☐ Learn to use the pleasant, unexpected response to motivate.

☐ Give your child a bucket and ask him or her to be a Thing Finder to pick up clutter around a room.

☐ Encourage your child to put his laundry away promptly by putting a note under it, redeemable for a surprise. You might include an expiration time.

☐ Take breaks during work time. A ten-minute family Frisbee game can be rejuvenating.

☐ Clean a cluttered room with a Penny-Flip Pick-Up. Flip a penny. If it lands on heads, pick up something to the right. If it lands on tails, then pick up and put away something on the left. It takes a little longer, but it can bring about laughter as workers end up going in circles.

☐ Offer a television picnic, complete with a tablecloth spread on the floor, as an incentive to complete a job.

☐ Reward your children by handing them a sack, plastic bag, or box filled with a craft project ready to be put together.

☐ Challenge children with the game Can You Make Your Bed Faster Than I Can Make Mine? If it doesn't work, try, "I'll help you; will you help me?"

☐ Pay for home jobs with play money and then hold an auction.

☐ Hide coins throughout a room to test thoroughness of a child's cleaning.

☐ Be aware of local or seasonal ideas and activities that might trigger incentives.

☐ Use marbles or other game tokens as a progress reward system. The reward is for the parent to play the game with the child when all the game pieces have been earned. For example: two marbles for making the bed, three marbles for sweeping the steps, and so forth.

☐ Keep a supply of gummed stickers to give as rewards such as school or music teachers put on a page after good effort—cute animals, nice sayings, hearts, or stars to wear on wrist or forehead.

☐ Have a birthday or anniversary party for your house. Encourage an extra-thorough cleaning, including minor repairs, small painting jobs, and the purchase of some household item. End the work with a special house-shaped cake and discussion of the accomplishments.

☐ Be the Servant for an Hour, to help a child finish up a tough chore, doing what the child requests.

☐ Leave a note on the table that reads, "Meet in the car at 2 P.M. and bring a note saying your chores are completed." Then take a trip to a swimming pool or ice-cream parlor. Make sure the work assigned can be completed in the scheduled time.

FEEDBACK

☐ Catch your child doing something right, instead of watching for him or her to do something wrong.

☐ Memorize five new positive phrases to use this week.

☐ Never redo a job that has been inspected and passed.

☐ Keep on the lookout for humor.

- [ ] Give the child a superhero name like Superman or Wonderwoman.
- [ ] Discipline without insulting.
- [ ] Look for something commendable to praise in each child every day.
- [ ] Entitle the child assigned to wash dishes a "pearl diver."
- [ ] Show interest and listen to your child's problems, whether large or small.
- [ ] Avoid negative labels. Children become what their parents and teachers expect them to become. Positive labels do more to convey love and motivate change.
- [ ] Build a child's self-esteem by expressing encouragement in these two parts: (a) tell how good it makes you feel, and (b) how it benefits the child and the family.
- [ ] Draw a picture of a house. Make it smiley or sad with a grease pencil, or attach a mouth with Scotch tape or Velcro, to use as a room or house barometer.
- [ ] Declare a special day called, You're It. This is a day to play tag by catching someone doing a helpful chore. The person caught is It and must catch someone else helping.
- [ ] Pick-It-Up-As-You-Go Club has the policy that if you use something, you put it away promptly. If not, membership is lost for a few days.
- [ ] Keep the evaluation pleasant.
- [ ] Give recognition for even meager accomplishments.
- [ ] Focus attention on effort made or lessons learned, not on merely the end result.
- [ ] Give recognition as soon as possible. Don't save up thanks.
- [ ] Ask, "How would you do this another time?"

- [ ] Let the child judge his or her own work.

- [ ] Request that the child restate instructions, to insure correct understanding.

- [ ] Make two pictures of the bedroom. The child can glue pictures of items on them so they look cluttered or neat. When the messy picture is taped on the door it means the room needs cleaning; the neat picture means the room is fine. Let the child be the judge.

JOB ASSIGNMENTS

- [ ] Let the children choose their own chores once in a while.

- [ ] Don't require as much work from the child when school is in session.

- [ ] Ask each child for one hour a day toward upkeep of the home: ten minutes in their own bedroom, fifteen minutes on a morning chore, fifteen minutes on an afternoon chore, and twenty minutes to help with dishes.

- [ ] Require two hours of work from the child on Saturday.

- [ ] Adjust chores, change requirements, and include children in decision making, as they mature.

- [ ] Help the child make a priority list of things he wants to do.

- [ ] Require some work from every child *every day.*

- [ ] Have a regular time each day to do chores.

- [ ] Try sending a "work request" through the U.S. mail, or make up your own in-house mail system. All children delight in receiving mail.

- [ ] Write the job on a slip of paper, crack open walnuts, insert the job slip, and reglue the shell together. Fun holiday job activity.

☐ Blow up a balloon, write the job on the outside of the balloon, then let the air out. Let children choose the balloon and blow it up to see what job they do.

☐ Slip rolled paper, with jobs written on them, into unfilled balloons. Blow up the balloons and let the children pop them to find jobs.

☐ Fill a "magic hat" with special work assignments or free-time suggestions.

☐ Seal the chore list in an envelope and let the family draw assignments as in a card game.

☐ Draw assignments from a basket or other interesting container.

☐ Roll dice to determine who does what job.

☐ Have a job treasure hunt.

☐ Follow a string to find the reward for a job well done.

CHORE CHARTS

☐ Try a weekly assignment chart to show who, what, and when.

☐ Screw cup hooks into a board and hang assignments written on marker tags.

☐ Make a "to do" list for the young child, to cross off basic grooming and chores for the day.

☐ Request that the child sign a written contract in agreement for a task as described on p. 61.

☐ Reinforce consistency and give immediate social rewards by using the Star Chart.

☐ Build an ice-cream sundae reward as incentive for good kitchen clean-up.

☐ Use the Race Car Chart for a two-week progress incentive. Make it like most game boards, with a car as a marker and a reward offered upon completion. This can also be displayed on the refrigerator door using colored tape and magnets.

☐ Draw a bean stalk and show the child progressing up the leaves as he follows through with an agreed-upon habit change.

☐ Set up a vertical chore chart for assigning one morning and one evening responsibility.

☐ Post chore charts in the kitchen, where they can be easily seen and referred to often.

☐ Use a circular chore chart to rotate jobs, especially in small families.

☐ Make flags on popsicle sticks to assign jobs, and keep them in individual cups.

☐ Draw a floor plan of your house and put a picture of the person in the room he or she is responsible for cleaning.

☐ Tie morning chore assignments onto breakfast spoons.

☐ Run off a stack of daily assignment charts, to be filled in each night for the following day.

☐ Write the children's first initials on the calendar, to rotate dishwashing or dog feeding.

☐ Write the after-dinner job on the napkin.

☐ Make a job-chart grid on poster board, then cover it with clear contact paper. Write in assignments with crayon that can easily be rubbed off with a soft cloth.

☐ Pin an "I Did It" badge on the young child after morning grooming and pick-up are finished.

MONEY

☐ Give children allowances so they can learn to manage money.

☐ Keep allowances small enough so that they don't meet all the growing wants as children enter their teens, thus providing incentive to earn more.

☐ Encourage children to take advantage of training classes for baby-sitting or first aid, and for proper care of equipment like the lawn mower or bicycle.

☐ Offer to pay the child for jobs you would normally pay someone else to do.

☐ Let older children help plan, select, and purchase their own clothes.

☐ Show the child where the family money goes by bringing home the paycheck in cash and then distributing the money into envelopes for each bill.

☐ Practice budgeting by planning the family vacation together.

☐ Have the child keep a log of his purchases and earnings.

☐ Help him start saving money for the future and open a savings account.

☐ Save money at home in a container that the child can see through.

☐ Let them count their money often if they want to do so.

☐ Pay for a job as soon as it is completed, especially in the beginning.

☐ Involve the children in some gift-giving decisions, even if they can't keep a secret.

SELF-ESTEEM

☐ Respect your child's right to privacy. Each of us wants to be alone sometimes.

☐ Teach family caring by establishing traditions. Holidays and birthdays are good markers for traditions. Regular family celebration is dear to a child.

☐ Watch for interest in your children that can be the basis for developing talents—things like cooking, music, art, and so forth—to increase feelings of self-worth.

☐ Showing love and respect to your spouse helps the child feel secure.

☐ Introduce your child to other people in a positive way when they stop to talk or visit.

☐ Tell your children often, in words and actions, that you love them. Don't assume they know.

☐ Recognize the child's worth and show respect. Knock before entering his/her room, and ask before using his/her possessions.

☐ Try to eat at least one meal a day together, as a family.

☐ Repeat traditions you enjoy together, to unite the family and nurture memories.

☐ Celebrate birthdays as a family to reinforce each child's feeling of importance.

☐ Make a crown out of paper, to remind your child how special he or she is to you. Let the child decorate and wear the crown.

☐ Avoid making continual threats or punishments. They seldom have permanent positive results.

☐ Correct a child privately rather than in front of friends or family, to save him/her from embarrassment.

☐ Create mail pockets for each family member in which to put "love notes" or assignments.

☐ Develop your own interests and talents. When children see your enthusiasm and growth it motivates and enriches their lives and serves as a model to try new things.

☐ Keep a list of "times when my kids were good helpers." Display the list where you and your children will often see it, to encourage such actions.

☐ Memorize positive mottoes as a family. For example: "God doesn't make junk!" or "Hook your wagon to a star."

☐ Plan opportunities for children to give compassionate service to someone in need. Such activities build love and appreciation, and more willingness to help at home.

☐ Share your talent, interests, and career with your children. Sometimes let them go with you to work, catch butterflies, or fish together. Just spend time doing things with each other.

☐ Give positive labels.

☐ Decorate a Sunshine Box with a slit in the top, in which to slip notes of appreciation, praise, or encouragement. "You brought sunshine into our home today by. . . ."

☐ Save some time for dreaming.

☐ Release tension by beginning to hum slowly and increasing to a loud scream. Done together with the family, this brings laughter.

☐ Say the word "freeze" to indicate quiet and motionlessness. Use it for a few seconds to calm a situation and then say "action."

☐ Give coupon books to your children with extra service or time together listed on the coupons. For example: "One free hour of reading with Mom or Dad" or "Two free bed-making jobs, at your request."

☐ Use some kind of signal, to show that emotions are strained, such as a red flag taped on the bedroom door or a hand signal.

☐ Remember that cooperation and mutual respect, not just getting the job done, is the goal.

☐ Celebrate firsts: first day at school, loss of first tooth, first snow of season and first day of summer. Celebrate Dad's or Mom's promotion or finished project; celebrate learning a new skill like riding a bicycle.

☐ Get out the scrapbooks when you feel discouraged. Look them over with a child and tell him or her the story of their birth and how you looked forward to their arrival, to build positive ground to start working on again.

FAMILY COUNCIL

☐ Listen, listen, listen.

☐ Allow your child to "speak his or her piece," airing complaints develops mutual understanding.

☐ Be thick-skinned.

☐ Take a few minutes at the beginning of family council for each person to express appreciation to the other family members.

☐ Toss a "hot" potato or a Nerf ball quickly from one to another until a buzzer rings. Then the person with the potato tells something nice about another family member.

☐ Do not set limits or make threats you cannot or are not willing to enforce.

☐ Don't let the telephone interrupt a family meeting, especially if you have teen-agers in your home.

☐ Be more consistent by letting children understand what is expected of them and by establishing some basic routines, for example, setting breakfast and dinner times and chore times.

☐ Set the rule, No one can do another's chores without permission from either Mother or Father.

☐ Leave a note to a busy teen asking for time (appointment) to discuss and get advice. The formality of the written note may help them give priority to the discussion and pay closer attention to the topic.

☐ Let the child pretend he is Newspaper Deliverer, to bring in the newspaper. Adult titles are fun.

☐ Give family members opportunities to initiate ideas, actions, and solutions, and remember to listen with openness.

☐ Coordinate schedules once a week, on a calendar located centrally in the house.

☐ Make a set of family rules and policies. Keep them positive.

☐ Agree on a household standard of cleanliness that suits your aesthetic needs and the amount of time that can be devoted to it. Also define purposes for which various rooms will be used.

☐ Take time for a private talk with your child, formally or informally, at least once every two months, alone.

☐ Treat children fairly but differently, according to interests and age.

☐ Put in writing the individual goals you want your child to work on for the next few months. The Home Progress Chart will give suggestions (see page 6).

CONSEQUENCES

☐ Allow the child free time to play.

☐ Use the principle "If this is not completed, we cannot move on to this."

☐ Carry through on consequences, but do so without anger, resentment, or retaliation.

☐ Don't withhold allowance money as punishment, unless it is a wage for work not completed.

☐ Let natural consequences happen, to teach respect for rules, self-control and fairness, as long as there is no danger to the child.

☐ Give support and comfort by saying, "You can do it" or "I am with you."

☐ Think over and explain ahead of time the consequences of misbehavior.

☐ Make a consequence reasonable and enforceable.

☐ Unplug the radio or lamp when a child forgets to turn it off. On the second offense, unplug it for a day.

☐ Charge a nickle whenever a light is left on.

☐ Set a limit: "This must be done before you next eat." This is only postponement, not withholding.

☐ Require repayment of a chore, for unnecessary service rendered by parent.

☐ Talk about the consequence, asking the child to restate the broken rule and tell how things could have been done better.

☐ Don't withhold a meal as punishment.

☐ Examine the relationship between parent and child for possible causes of problems.

☐ Don't let the punishment exceed the child's tolerance for accepting it.

☐ Create a "time out" corner or spot for short visits when the child needs to get control. Five or ten minutes in this spot is usually long enough; an hour is definitely too long.

☐ Change the consequence if it is too powerful.

☐ Ask the child for an opinion as to what discipline should be given. This reduces feelings of resentment toward the parent. It may mean bartering for the appropriate solution, but a child's own ideas seem fairer to him.

TEACH THE JOB

☐ Use clear, simple instructions, especially with a young child.

☐ Stop work while it's still fun. Don't drag it out just because you have good workers.

☐ Show and express your own positive attitudes about your work.

☐ Offer clear, firm, friendly insistence on proper performance.

☐ Do not assume that a child knows *how* to do something, even if she has watched you do it.

☐ Act rather than react. When we act, we control our behavior; when we react, we allow circumstances to control us.

☐ Consider the individual differences in children.

☐ Remember that handicapped children should also be given responsibilities.

☐ Break the job down into small, manageable parts.

☐ Thoroughly show and tell each part of a job.

☐ Stay with the child as he works until he has successfully completed a chore three different times on separate days.

☐ Say at least two positive things about the job every time it is completed especially in the beginning.

☐ Tell the child how long she will have to work so she can see the end.

☐ Keep work periods short and successful.

☐ Give advance notice of approaching work days.

☐ Work before fun. Reinforce less enjoyable activity with a preferred activity: "After this is done, you can do this."

☐ Spend part of work time teaching preventative actions such as taking shoes and boots off before tracking into the house to save on clean-up. Wash hands after eating to save from having smudges on walls and furniture.

☐ Give a five-minute warning before play time is over, to let children gear down and prepare for work time.

☐ Teach efficiency such as making one trip to the bedroom carrying four items instead of four trips carrying one item each time.

☐ Use the terms "right" and "left" with your child early to help him learn to follow directions.

☐ Teach aesthetics while working. Enjoy the pleasure of making things attractive and beautiful. Let children be a part of pretty things like fresh flowers.

☐ Guide a child into discovering for himself what still needs to be done by asking questions. "What needs to be done next in your bedroom?" is better than saying, "Now pick up your dirty clothes."

☐ Leave the responsibility with the child by asking, "Would you like me to help? What would you like me to do?"

☐ Allow individual interpretation of how the job is to be done by asking for the child's opinions.

☐ Start a Finger Play for Chores for children from two and a half years to seven (see page 86).

☐ Teach practical work processes like washing dishes from right to left (or vice versa) so clean dishes end up near cupboard storage to save unnecessary work motions.

☐ Help the child when he asks for it.

☐ Be available to supervise.

☐ Offer encouragement and appreciation often when teaching a task.

☐ Pull back on your demands during a child's stressful times.

☐ Re-evaluate assignments often.

☐ Assign a color to each family member. Color-code items such as toothbrushes and cups by using colored markers. Clothing items can be coded by attaching a scrap of fabric with a small safety pin. This makes it easier for a child to sort items.

☐ Make the child believe this job is possible, not by telling him how easy the job is but by building his confidence in himself.

☐ Draw on the child's past successes as a positive model.

☐ Don't compare the child to siblings or friends.

☐ Emphasize the good and not the bad progress of the job.

☐ Discuss improving methods without attacking the personality, being specific about details of the task.

☐ Write down the job specifications for rooms and jobs. Tack them in closets or behind curtains in the appropriate rooms (see page 84).

☐ Advise rather than command, especially after the child is twelve years old.

☐ Respect the free agency of each family member by letting him make his own decisions so far as his stage of development will allow.

☐ Keep the choices offered to a young child simple, and usually not more than two choices.

☐ Try to force your children and you may fail, but if you are willing to take the time to give loving guidance, your chances of succeeding are greatly multiplied.

☐ Speak the child's name first so she knows you are talking to her.

☐ Consider safety factors when making assignments.

☐ Speak in a soft, calm voice.

☐ Picture your child and yourself succeeding in your mind—you have to believe it can happen.

☐ Watch for spontaneous teaching moments.

☐ Have special lessons with names like Sew-on-Button Night (teach everyone to sew on buttons), or try Sort Dirty Clothes or Sew Patches on Blue Jeans.

☐ Give explanations, instead of saying, "Do this because I say so."

☐ Show, pleasantly and firmly, that you mean what you say.

☐ Once you have asked that a thing be done, follow up.

☐ Call everyone together for a clean-the-bathtub-or-tile lesson. Divide the tile into sections with masking tape and assign each person a different section. Don't be surprised if everyone gets wet.

☐ Make "magic eye glasses" from construction paper. Go on a hunt for places germs grow—inside drains, garbage disposal, bottoms of wastebaskets, and the can opener.

☐ Act out a lesson. Dress up as Miss Litter Bug to teach about cleanliness and order.

☐ Organize a "maid basket" with basic, safe cleaning supplies, to be taken into the room that is to be cleaned.

☐ Show how to work from visible areas of a room to out-of-sight areas, such as making the bed and picking up clothes before cleaning out the drawers.

☐ Pick up biggest things first, then smaller items.

☐ Work in a clockwise direction around the room.

☐ Schedule pick-up time after each play period and just before eating or going to bed.

☐ Have the child dress, comb hair, brush teeth, and put on shoes before working.

☐ Paint the dull edge of a knife with colored fingernail polish so children can help with meals safely by being able to distinguish easily between edges.

☐ Give models. Show and tell how to do something to make doing it easier, thus building confidence.

☐ Teach a skill. A skill is a gift that lasts forever, whereas other toys and games last only a short time.

☐ Let your children take part in learning fun skills, not just janitorial tasks. Some examples are decorating a cake, planning games for a birthday party, arranging flowers, buying treats, or filling the bird feeder.

EVALUATION

☐ Be sure you have taught every detail of the job, not leaving any gaps of assumed understanding.

☐ Try a fifty-point inspection sheet to evaluate a bedroom (see page 150).

☐ Evaluate the room based on its condition before the job was started rather than on what still must be done. Then compare it with the established standard.

☐ Deal only with the present circumstance and shun words like never, always, and every time.

☐ Go through the house twice a day at eight o'clock to pick up items left out and put them in an Extra Service Box. Redemption comes by doing a make-up chore or by paying a "service charge."

☐ Be understanding of stress and outside pressures from school work, teachers, coaches, or peers.

☐ Repeat a request over and over (broken-record technique) in a calm unemotional manner when a stituation can no longer be tolerated and must be confronted.

☐ Don't be intimidated by what friends or relatives think your child should do. Work with your child and make your own plan.

☐ Make a change if the child can't handle the job.

☐ Cool off when you are angry, before taking action.

☐ Do not compare one child with another.

☐ Attack the problem, not the child.

☐ Don't expect a child to do everything to adult standards.

☐ Keep a list for a week of incidences when harmony and unity were disrupted. Analyze the time of day and who was involved. Then decide on ways to make changes in the circumstances.

☐ Take a few minutes weekly to individually assess your effectiveness as a parent. Praise yourself for progress and make commitments for any needed changes.

☐ Hide a tape recorder and record some candid family conversations, then let the people involved objectively evaluate where to make improvements. Children often do not realize how much they complain, and parents often do not realize how demanding and negative they can sound.

☐ Analyze the time of day when successes happen and then capitalize on it.

☐ Don't harp on small imperfections.

☐ Evaluate by role playing. When jobs are poorly done, let the child play the part of the parent and the parent make excuses as the child normally does. Ask the child what he would say and do as a parent to bring about more harmony and understanding.

☐ Avoid "do it or else" situations.

PERSONAL ORGANIZATION

☐ Develop the "bag habit," to keep school notices and library books organized (see page 222).

☐ Purchase an alarm clock for each child when they start school, to develop personal responsibility for getting themselves up each morning.

☐ Help your child set weekly goals to curtail procrastination, increase productivity, and limit forgetfulness.

☐ Give your children their own calendars, and help them write in all the birthdays of friends and relatives at the beginning of the year.

☐ Locate the homework study area away from distractions of television and younger children.

☐ Mount an outside thermometer where it can be seen from inside the house. Encourage the child to read it, and to make his or her own decision as to whether a coat and hat are needed that day.

GENERAL ORGANIZATION

☐ Keep bikes and wagons in their place by painting parking lines on the cement floor of the garage or patio.

☐ Label records and record jackets by drawing matching pictures on each of them. This way young children can keep them put away properly.

☐ Encourage children to buy birthday gifts for friends ahead of time, at sales. Having a small gift supply on hand teaches organization of time, effort, and money.

☐ Create a drop-off spot near your entranceway for library books, school books, and briefcases.

☐ Hang a multipocket shoe bag on the inside of a closet door to hold small toys, stocking caps, mittens, socks, or slippers.

☐ Sort toys into several different boxes and give your children a different box every few days, to rotate their toys and maintain their interest.

☐ Cut down on taking boots off and putting them back on, by providing plastic bags by the back door to be slipped over boots when a quick trip into the house is necessary.

☐ Large vegetable and fruit boxes and laundry baskets can serve as files or drawers on a shelf.

☐ Help your young child make a clock out of a paper plate, and discuss when play, chore, and bed times are to be. This helps them understand an orderly schedule.

☐ Post messages at a specific spot in your home, perhaps by the kitchen phone or at the back door.

☐ Organize a place for toys—either all together in one room or in appropriate areas for different types of play. Avoid storing toys in the following areas: master bedroom, living room, or stairs.

☐ Use shelf dividers and drawer compartments made from cardboard boxes or purchased.

☐ Store bathtub toys in a bag made from nylon mesh. Hang it with a shower curtain clip from the faucet or towel rack.

☐ Stand back and evaluate where toys are used, especially after a hard play session. Sometimes, it is better to rearrange and store toys in the places where the children use them the most.

☐ Use sheets of cork, foam-backed outdoor carpet squares, or peg board for bulletin boards.

☐ Provide a large trash barrel (with lid) outside in which to store outside toys like trucks, buckets, balls, etc.

☐ Install hooks within a child's reach for hanging coats and sweaters.

☐ Make a place for crayons, pencils, markers, rulers, and so forth by putting empty soup cans in a sixpack soda pop carrier. Gluing a piece of cardboard to the underside and painting it with latex wall paint will make it sturdier.

☐ Pin socks together before tossing them into the laundry to save on sorting and lost socks.

☐ Use small trunks or suitcases to store things.

☐ Set aside a corner or cupboard for art and craft supplies, and provide a table or counter where children are free to paint, paste, or cut.

☐ Hang model airplanes from the ceiling with fishing line and thumbtacks to help clear space on a shelf.

☐ Keep a supply of paper and pencils on hand at a specific location, for homework needs.

☐ Have a specific place to keep schoolbooks. Even a box behind the sofa is better than having them scattered everywhere.

☐ Hang a mug rack on the wall. Sew loops on stuffed animals to hook over each mug peg.

☐ Buy clip hooks (similar to what you hang brooms on) for closets, to hold tennis rackets, bats, etc.

☐ Use plastic dish pans as terrific dividers for toys and craft projects. They are easy to carry from place to place.

☐ Sew pieces of Velcro (fabric tape that sticks to itself) to a long strip of cloth and hang it on the wall. Sew corresponding pieces of Velcro to stuffed animals and store them by sticking them to the cloth strip.

☐ Purchase plastic vegetable bins that can be stacked and easily seen through for storage of magazines, clothes, or toys.

KITCHEN

☐ Store dinnerware where the child can reach it, to be able to set the table without help from the parent.

☐ "Put your own dishes in the dishwasher and scrub two pots and pans or serving dishes, and Dad or Mom will do what's left" is the Olness family dishwashing agreement.

☐ Let one child at a time go with you to help with grocery shopping.

☐ Give your child ten dollars and let him plan, shop for, and prepare a family dinner.

☐ Post dinner menus weekly so older children can start dinner before you get home from work.

☐ Buy a smaller broom to accommodate a small child.

☐ Send your child to Grandma's to learn to make bread or cookies from the "pro."

☐ Keep coupons together by helping your children decorate a box, make a slit in the top, and store collected coupons in the box until they can be sorted.

☐ Let the child play waiter or waitress and prepare the orders for simple lunch or breakfast meals.

☐ Make a silhouette of a single place setting on a place mat for the young child to use as an example when setting the table. The picture should include plate, glass, knife, fork, spoon, and napkin.

☐ Ways to interest and motivate your child to cook:

• Make up interesting and fun names for food such as Yankee Doodle Beef instead of macaroni and hamburger.

• Teach children to make funny faces on top of dry cereal or on cottage cheese for salad with pieces of fresh or dried fruit.

• Cut sandwiches from several kinds of breads into different shapes (triangles, circles, etc.) or from cookie cutters. Use a variety of fillings; even make a three-layer sandwich.

• Make an egg in a frame by tearing out or cutting a hole in a piece of bread, setting it in the fry pan, pouring egg into the hole and frying it.

• Let the child pick out a special mold for gelatin salad.

• Create brownie turtles by dropping spoonfuls of brownie batter or thick cake mix in the center of five nuts arranged in a circle, then bake.

☐ Decrease work time by making several sandwiches ahead of time and storing them in the freezer. This can be a family project for lunch preparations that save time for everyone.

☐ Let the child work alongside the adult during meal preparations.

☐ Purchase a recipe box for each child in which to keep the recipes he or she likes and successfully learns to make.

☐ Have your child prepare one dish successfully several times before assigning an entire meal.

☐ Set the policy that those who cook clean up after themselves, but don't have to do the general dishes for that meal.

☐ Present the Jiggle-Joggle-Jell-O Award or the Magnificent Marvelous Meatloaf Award after those foods have been successfully prepared.

☐ Show your children how to break down dinner preparations into blocks of time, working backward from the time when dinner is to be served.

☐ Give a new cookbook as a gift.

☐ Enroll your children in community and school cooking classes.

☐ Have a pretend restaurant, using play money and leaving a tip. Clean-up is more fun when using a tray and maybe a cart, if you have one.

☐ Assign a Cook for the Day with the parent serving as assistant.

BEDROOM ORGANIZATION

☐ Help the child create a place for everything.

☐ Add something new to the child's room from time to time to spark interest.

☐ Roll children's clothing or fold it small to store it vertically in drawers like books on a shelf rather than stack it on top of reach other.

☐ Include children in throw-out decisions after they are five or six years old.

☐ A messy room for several days signals a need for parental help in cleaning and organizing.

☐ Play a two-point game by tossing each item of soiled clothing into the hamper.

☐ Sit on the floor in the middle of the child's bedroom for thirty minutes and brainstorm ways to cut down the quantity of items and to arrange items so that everything has a place.

☐ Help the child keep items in the bedroom to a manageable number by providing a place to store treasures and keepsakes and by helping get rid of unneeded extras.

☐ Teach the young child how to make a bed by having her crawl in, pull the blankets up, and then slither out.

☐ Provide bedcovers and a spread that are easy for the child to make up, or plan on helping the child make the bed every day.

☐ Rearrange the furniture as you thoroughly clean to give a feeling of cleanness and a desire to keep it looking nice.

☐ Store pajamas under the bed pillow or in the pillowcase.

☐ Create a bag for soiled laundry from an old favorite T-shirt. Sew the bottom of the shirt and the arm holes together and slip in a coathanger from the top. Clothes go in through the neck hole.

☐ Cut out silhouettes of shoes from contact paper and stick them on the shelf or closet floor to show where the shoes belong.

☐ Purchase a drawer organizer, such as is commonly used for nails and screws, for the child who collects small things.

☐ Separate toys into bags or boxes, rather than have them dumped into one large toy box where everything gets mixed up.

☐ Place a large bucket in a closet corner to hold items such as bats and balls.

☐ Store toy bags on a game tree, which is like a coat tree but with hooks all the way down the pole.

☐ Make elastics or giant rubber bands for boxes to keep them closed in case they get dropped.

☐ Hang animals and dolls with ribbons tied around their necks on a long wooden rod (two-inch diameter) hung vertically from a plant hook in the ceiling.

☐ Place treasures and keepsakes where younger brothers and sisters or playmates won't get them.

☐ Let your child learn to manage a few things well by setting limits on papers, toys, and clothes.

☐ Make portable bookcases or shelves from bricks and boards. Cinderblocks make larger divisions for hobbies, and tables, desks, or even room dividers. Spaces between the shelves can be made from anything—logs, stone slabs, or boxes—if they can support the weight.

☐ Arrange furniture around the walls to create maximum floor space for play or work activities.

☐ Use boxes for hundreds of things and in many places to make better use of shelves and drawers. Covering them with contact paper makes them pleasing to the eye and more durable.

☐ Use cold-cereal boxes as organizers for magazines.

☐ Have a container in every bedroom to serve as a clothes hamper.

☐ Make drawer dividers with shoe boxes to separate socks, underwear, belts, and pajamas.

☐ Provide, for the child who is old enough to hang up his clothes, a clothes rod that is low enough for him to reach.

☐ Keep currently worn clothes separated from out-of-season or out-of-size clothes.

☐ Fasten a towel rod on the back of a swinging closet door, for hanging bulky items like snowsuits.

☐ Put a wastebasket in every room. The living room might be the exception.

☐ Label shelves and drawers in children's rooms, storage areas, work areas, and the kitchen. Helps children know where to return a borrowed item.

☐ Organize every chest of drawers the same way for each young family member: top drawer, treasures; second drawer, pajamas; third drawer, socks and underclothes; and so forth. This makes putting clothes away quicker and easier.

☐ Make it an annual tradition to clean out the drawers and use the wrapping paper from the child's birthday gifts to line the drawers.

☐ Hang a broomstick from the clothes rod in the closet with two ropes to increase the rod space for short items like pants or shirts. This doubles the space available for clothing of younger children.

☐ Provide a place for books in the bedroom to help the child keep books in neat order. It also develops the reading habit.

Appendix A
Helping the Child Get Organized for School

Have your children, like ours, lost school notices, or misplaced homework assignments, or forgotten to return their field trip permission slips? There are ways you can help smooth the school experience, not only helping the child to be a better student and feel better about himself, but also stretching the time available for family help and fun.

Marie Crawford explained that those children who are good organizers know better when and how to do what. Organization training for school begins in kindergarten. When Becky McCullough was five, her teacher encouraged the "bag habit" by asking each student to bring a backpack or a cloth or plastic bag with handles to school each day. The children put notes to parents, finished work, permission slips, and library books in their bags, to be taken home at the end of the day. The McCulloughs knew where to find schoolwork and messages and where to place items to be returned to school. At home, school materials were not scattered about the minute Becky walked in the door. Rather the "bag" was hung on a hook in her closet until the items could be sorted. The bag habit gave Becky a sense of confidence in her ability to handle the school experience. During her teaching years, Sue Monson has seen many children in tears because of a lost homework assignment or forgotten permission slip. Most children take school seriously and want to succeed at it. Knowing school supplies are organized lessens the feeling of anxiety and builds self-reliance and self-confidence.

The Allred family made their children responsible for getting up and off to school without parental prodding. The family tradition was to purchase an alarm clock as a gift for each child when they started school. If the child had difficulty getting up, the alarm clock was the bad guy, not the parent. The teachers at one junior high provided a sheet for each student to record their grades from tests, labs, homework, and class assignments. The students placed the tally sheets in the fronts of their notebooks and recorded their grades; they always knew exactly where they stood. You can help your child incorporate this same system—it saves the "surprise" at report card time.

High school students who maintain a part-time job, participate in choir, band, athletics or other extracurricular activities, in addition to their regular class load, need special help in organizing their time and energy. One senior found a pocket calendar her solution; she carefully checked it before committing to any project. Such a calendar can be a valuable aid to the busy teen-ager.

Helping your child set weekly school goals curtails procrastination, increases productivity, and limits forgetfulness. Many school assignments known well in advance are still put off until the last minute; weekly spelling or vocabulary tests, Friday quizzes, term papers, and the "poster" report are examples. The following chart was designed for recording school commitments and other activities like music lessons, athletic practices and games, or appointments. Have the child list the "Things I Have to Do" and the "Things I Want to Do" then fit them into the days of the week. After using these sheets for a month, Sidney, a high school sophomore, commented, "My life revolves around homework, and this chart helped me write

Week of _____

Things I Have to Do	Things I Want to Do
Monday	Tuesday
Wednesday	Thursday
Friday	Saturday/Sunday

everything down in one place and not forget it. It kept me organized."

Who is responsible for homework? You will hear conflicting opinions from school experts; some saying, "It's the child's job entirely and parents should not intefere," others responding with, "Parents should see that the child gets the homework done, no matter what." You probably have had both ideas thrust at you, either directly or indirectly, from your child's teachers. You can be made to feel like it is your fault if homework assignments are late or not done. The following sensible,

HOW TO HELP YOUR CHILDREN DO
THEIR HOMEWORK
AND DEVELOP GOOD STUDY HABITS

1. Ask if they have homework.
2. Be interested in what they are doing.
3. Don't get upset with them, especially if they have trouble with the subject.
4. Help them set aside short periods of time to study, rather than one long period.
5. If they cannot figure out how to do an assignment on their own, go over it with them, tell them *how,* but don't supply the answers.
6. Have a time and place set aside for doing homework away from distractions of television and younger children.
7. Keep school supplies like paper and pencils on hand.
8. Provide a specific place to keep school books.

---

middle-of-the-road suggestions compiled by a group of administrators and teachers from Lansing Christian Schools in Lansing, Michigan, are offered for your consideration.

Homework is the child's responsibility but a supportive parent makes the responsibility easier to carry—just as a parent's employment is easier if a child cooperates in helping with household responsibilities. Peer influence in drug use, early dating, and other undesirable behavior is strong. If the child doesn't find satisfaction from doing a good job at school, the chance of following these influences increases as the child searches for something to give that "I belong" feeling.

Create an environment where learning is convenient, providing not only a location (desk or table), good lighting and supplies, but also a parent availability to discuss and support. A quiet homework hour can be the perfect time for the parent to catch up on personal reading. Parents who read tend to have children who read. A bulletin board to display reports and art projects is enjoyed as much by older children as by younger ones. You might put a clothes line down a stairway wall for a unique way to hang schoolwork.

The questioning technique is useful in helping your child organize for school. "What homework do you have tonight?" "How long do you think it will take?" "Did you have any special plans for after your homework?" These questions help the child set goals. It may also help to write down assignments as soon as they get home from school—a visual reminder of what must be done. All the encouraging and questioning will not be necessary daily. But with an established time and place for doing homework and a parent's support, the child is more likely to get the "homework first" habit.

Appendix B
Helping the Child Begin Cooking

Food excites almost everyone, especially children. As a child, Sue Monson remembers a comment from a man who walked into their messy kitchen while she and several friends were mixing up cookies. "I'd give anything if my wife would let our kids do this. She says it's too much bother." When a college student, new bride, or groom takes over cooking responsibilities, their success is related to the amount of exposure they have had to cooking in the past. Even the knowledge of how to prepare five main dishes can be a springboard to a variety of other menu ideas. The confidence gained from those few meals can make the first adjustment bearable, even enjoyable.

How can you help your child learn basic cooking skills? Involve them in your everyday food preparations. One of the daily chore assignments should be titled Assistant Cook. The child can work alongside the adult in dinner preparations, or the adult could be the assistant to the child and do things his or her way. Assign someone to fix Sunday morning breakfast or Saturday lunch. (Take time for advance preparations so the child can help plan the menu and make sure the ingredients are available.) Two preteen daughters were charged with the job of fixing dinner every Thursday night while Mom was teaching Cub Scouts. Another mother in Canada used the recipe-box incentive. She gave each of her teen-agers (boy and girl) a recipe box for Christmas, with a promise to copy every recipe they successfully learned to make. As each child left home, they took their collection of tried-and-liked recipes with them, along with a confident feeling and a box of warm memories.

Remember that experience has made you very efficient. A meal you can prepare and have on the table in an hour may take two or three times that long for a child. Avoid a frustrating experience by planning ample time. Have your child prepare one dish successfully several times before assigning an entire meal. Then, if you do give them full responsibility for a meal, don't criticize their efforts or the results. Every cook has made numerous embarrassing mistakes. Let your children learn from their experiences so they can build pride and confidence.

Show your children how to break down dinner preparations into blocks of time. For example, if baking potatoes takes an hour, put those in before cooking the green beans, that take only ten minutes. Working backward from the time dinner is to be on the table helps clarify just how long the preparations will take. Always allow a cushion of time for interruptions or errors.

Children like the policy "Those who cook do not have to clear the table or wash the dishes." This does not mean they are excused from cleaning up as they cook. Straightening and putting things back is part of preparation. For example, making a cake includes putting away ingredients, washing mixing utensils, and wiping the counter. However, the child who cooks a meal appreciates being excused from washing dinnerware.

Special recognition awards add sparkle. Present the Jiggle-Joggle-Jell-O Award or the Magnificent Marvelous Meatloaf Award after those foods have been successfully prepared.

Awards can be made simply of paper and ribbon. If you hold a family council, present the awards at that time with much fanfare and display them prominently somewhere, where the proud owners can get pleasure from seeing them.

One mother collects all the ingredients for cookies or a cake, spreads them out on the kitchen table, and covers them with a cloth. When her children finish their morning chores, they get to uncover the ingredients and either help her make the goodies or make them themselves. The element of surprise helps the children buzz through their morning chores to get the reward of a cooking experience.

Measuring techniques need to be taught early. Teach a child the difference between using a measuring cup (glass) for liquids, checking at eye level to meet the correct line, and using the dry-measure cups for very thick or dry ingredients. The dry-measure cups need to be leveled off with a straight-edge. As our country makes more use of the metric system we all will need to pay closer attention to metric or standard measurements in recipes. Charlie made the mistake of filling the glass measuring cup to ¼ liter (almost 1 cup) instead of ¼ cup. The blueberry pancake batter looked like eggnog.

Children can start using recipes after learning a few measuring techniques. Make sure they understand some basic cooking definitions before turning them loose. The following list might be a good beginning:

Bake:	use of oven to cook (called *roasting* for meats).
Beat:	mix rapidly to make a mixture smooth (use spoon, wire whip, eggbeater, or electric mixer).
Blend:	mix several ingredients together until smooth and uniform.
Boil:	cook (usually on top of the stove) until a mixture bubbles rapidly.
Brown:	cook food over high heat until it becomes brown in color.
Chop:	cut into pieces.

Cream: beat until soft and fluffy.

Dice: cut food into small sizes.

Fry: cook in a small amount of oil on top of stove (same as *sautéing*).

Grate: rub food on a grater to make little pieces (sometimes called *shred*).

Grease: smear or rub shortening in a pan (like a cake pan) to prevent food from sticking.

Mix: stir together.

Simmer: heat until bubbles just break the surface.

Whip: beat rapidly until it expands and gets thick.

There are many fun recipes children can successfully prepare with the understanding of the above. Some beginning foods could include these:

cinnamon toast	flavored drinks
stuffed celery	frozen orange juice
garlic bread	sandwiches
gelatin salad	fruit salad (canned fruit)
banana splits	hot dogs
eggnog	soup (canned or dry)
soft/hard-boiled eggs	macaroni and cheese
scrambled eggs	pizza
French toast	tearing lettuce for tossed salad
hot beverages	preparing potatoes for baking

Most bookstores have a wide selection of cookbooks especially designed for the beginning young cook. These make excellent gifts.

There are community groups and individuals who can also help teach cooking skills. The 4-H organization offers an excellent program in food preparation from preschool through high school. Grandparents seem to have the magic touch and golden patience when it comes to delicious recipes and cooking techniques. Elicit this help.

Even if you don't enjoy cooking, you have probably managed to fix nutritious meals with relative ease. Teach these basic skills to your children. One woman reflects about a college roommate, Pat, who had a turn to cook once a week, a dreaded time for the five other girls sharing the apartment. Besides spending four times more money than they did, Pat also spent the entire afternoon in preparing the meal and all evening cleaning up the mess. She came to school without the knowledge of how to make even one meal. Giving your children an opportunity to cook at home will help them avoid this type of experience.

Appendix C
Helping the Child Know the Neighborhood and City

On a cold, rainy night in September, Heather, a young adult, left a friend's house at twelve-thirty for the twenty-minute ride home. She drove in circles, getting farther away from home for three and one half hours. Twice she stopped to ask directions from police officers, only to get more confused. At 4 A.M. the telephone rang at her home with the distressed cry of "Help, I'm lost!" She received simple directions to follow familiar roads and to stop and call if she got lost again. Spending her last two dollars for gas at an all-night service station, she headed home. But the forty minutes it should have taken her expanded into another four hours. Confused again and not understanding how to use the increasing or decreasing street numbers as a guide, she drove until she ran out of gas, fell asleep in the cold car, and was awakened by a stranger. He took her in his truck to buy her a little gas, and pointed her in the right direction. She was now only a few miles from home. Luckily, her encounter with the stranger was a favorable one, but this totally frustrating and traumatic experience for this twenty-year-old could have been avoided with early training in navigation skills.

How can you help your children develop a sense of direction and understand how to read a map? You may think map reading is a natural talent that some individuals have while others do not. However, that idea is usually an excuse that really means "Let someone else find the way, I'm along for the ride." A few basics in map reading will not only be helpful but will give a boost to your children's confidence.

Shouldn't the schools teach map-reading skills? Yes, and they do, but usually in a very general manner and with limited time and little, if any, "on-the-street" training. Locating the directions north, south, east, and west in a workbook is different from turning children loose to find their way on the streets of a large city. Use the direction words as well as the names of the streets near you when talking with your children. When your toddler builds roads in sand and dirt piles with make-believe towns, use this beginning interest to build more detailed understanding. To help children recognize the layout of your streets, a map of your community can be drawn on a large piece of fabric with magic markers. As the children play with cars, trucks, animals, and people along the named streets they are starting map reading.

Many parents find that children have a keen desire to know the neighborhood. Teaching time invested early might save the worry associated with a lost child! Make walking or driving around the streets where you live a learning experience by pointing out significant landmarks like churches, schools, or different styles or colors of houses. Talk about the names of the streets and the way the houses are numbered. It is surprising how many ten-year-olds cannot name the streets two or three blocks from their homes.

As the child gets older, any trip in the car can hold a teaching moment. "Which direction are we going?" "Notice the numbers on the street markers. Are we getting farther away or nearer to the center of town?" Give your children practice being navigators when going on a special family excursion like to the zoo. Supply them with a map and drive only where they tell you. Encourage use of words like turn north or south rather than words like turn right or left.

Try some one-time navigation lessons at home. Draw up a simple floor plan of your house. (This could also be used for your fire/emergency escape drills.) Give directions like "Turn east at the second door down the hall and find a surprise on the bed." A map of your yard can be drawn and used for pickup, lawn-mowing, and weed-pulling assignments. Joyce Frank, a second grade teacher, devised a one-page map of the streets around the school for her students to use. Most of them lived in the mapped area, making it fun to locate the streets where friends lived as well as learn the layout of the neighborhood. You might sketch a map of your neighborhood, hide a treasure somewhere in the area, call your children adventurous pirates, and send them on a treasure hunt. This makes a fun learning experience for a birthday or slumber party.

When moving to a new town, one family found it invaluable to tape a map of the city up on the kitchen wall for several weeks. Each time they traveled to a new place in the city they marked the map and followed the route from their house to their destination. It didn't take long for everyone to become familiar with the major streets and the general locations of shopping centers, doctors, and other spots of interest.

Children living in rural communities may not need the same knowledge of road maps that a city dweller must have. But chances are small of a child staying "down on the farm" forever. A trip to a city a few times, with emphasis on orientation skills, can be a meaningful experience and build confidence for later years.

Understanding how to read a map is also a benefit when riding public transit systems. A taxi cab driver isn't as likely to take advantage of you by running up extra miles if you know your way around, and you won't be getting off the bus a mile *after* the dental office. When your children ride the bus to a new destination, give them a list of the major street names. They can watch for the street just before their stop and ring the buzzer in time to get off. (Make sure they understand the signal used to notify the bus driver to pull over.) If you have access to a subway, you know it can be a monster, even for an experienced traveler. Go with your children until they become very familiar with the route they must take. Encourage them to ride the subway with a friend the first few times they go without you. At least, if there is an unpleasant experience of getting lost, it can be shared! Even though the potential for frustration is high, there is also a very exhilarating feeling when one has successfully made a trip and arrived at the right spot at the right time.

Working parents who are not always available to drive their children from an athletic event to a piano lesson, to a friend's house, and so on, often give their children the advantage of more exposure to the public transit system. Confidence and independence develop as children cope with these experiences.

Exposure is the key. Take advantage of the places you already go, and use the maps you already have to build your child's awareness of his or her surroundings. Taking time to teach your children while they are with you can avoid a repeat of Heather's experience of getting lost.

Appendix D
Helping the Child Explore and Plan a Career

"What should I be when I grow up?" Your children's future careers will affect them as well as you. If you tell your children what to be and they later decide against your wishes, they feel they have disappointed you. If they become what you want but don't enjoy it, then they resent you. Your responsibility is not to say, "Be a teacher!" or "Be a plumber!," but rather to give guidance in helping them (1) know themselves, (2) explore and compare careers, and (3) decide a way to reach their goals.

KNOWING THEMSELVES

Insights about your children are clues to career possibilities. Your child may like to tinker with things, pulling them apart, putting them together again, or building something new. Another child may thrive on working out a monthly budget or figuring the square footage of the lawn in preparation to buying fertilizer, and still another child may want to be surrounded by friends every minute—a real conversationalist and

236

social butterfly. A people-oriented person probably would find a job as a research scientist as confining as the data-oriented person would find a job as a hotel manager.

Parents hear children fantasize about what they would like to be. If Johnny, at seven, talks about being a football star, let him enjoy his fantasy even if you see that as a very unlikely role for him. However, at twelve, if he still talks about being a football hero but shows absolutely no promise on the little league football team, you can begin drawing some realism into his dream. Ask, "Why do you think this would be exciting? What else would you like to be, if for some reason you couldn't be a football player?" Don't make an issue of what seem to be unrealistic choices, because career decisions don't need to be made at twelve.

Provide a broad base of experiences. Take your children places and encourage them to join clubs and have hobbies. City recreation departments and community organizations offer varied programs to meet a child's interests—direct them in these areas. Try to eliminate sex bias in thinking about experiences to provide. If a friend tells your daughter that she can only be a nurse and not a doctor, try to acquaint her with a female doctor or a male nurse. Point out that her desire and ability are more important than her sex. Notice, and give praise for, the school subjects in which your children excel. Teach them that their "job" as students—getting to school on time and completing assignments accurately—is important for a successful career in the future.

Your job as a parent involves helping your child develop a positive attitude about working. One high school counselor said the number one complaint from employers is "Why can't you teach kids to have a positive attitude?" If, as parents, you see your role as contributing to society, your child will likely pick up that attitude, too.

The opportunities and attitude you provide will help your children build faith in themselves, foster a feeling of worth, and find what really interests them. By the time they are about seventeen they should be in a better position to honestly answer "What do I really enjoy? What life style is for me?"

EXPLORING AND COMPARING CAREERS

If you know yourself, you can better explore and compare careers. When Charlene, a high school junior, could only talk about the excitement of ranch life and horse training as a career, her parents arranged an experience for her on a dude ranch. After feeding, brushing, saddling, and scooping up after the horses all summer, Charlene decide ranch life was not very romantic, and she was ready to look at other career choices. Where can you send your children for guidance? Have them ask people about their jobs, and visit job sites to provide still a broader understanding. Lori was determined to be a nurse, until she visited a small clinic and passed out from the smell of the anesthetic. Many high schools provide career exploration programs that can answer your child's questions about the employment outlook for the future, suggest some suitable career options for your child's academic strengths and weaknesses, and give aptitude tests that analyze interests and skills. Of course, these tests won't tell your child what to be, but they will offer hints and guidance toward possible fields. School counselors can offer job interview tips, suggestions for filling out resumés, and supply current books and magazines about different careers.

Some high schools may not offer career guidance so you are on your own to find help. A good source to begin with is the *Occupational Outlook Handbook,* published by the U.S. Department of Labor, Bureau of Labor Statistics. It is revised and reissued every two years and copies are available at most libraries. It gives job qualifications, salaries, opportunities for employment, and present trends in thousands of careers.

The Boy Scouts of America offer a career program, Explorer Scouts, for boys and girls between the ages of fourteen and twenty-one. As a parent you can call the Scout office in your community and tell them the career in which your child is interested, from *A*viation to *Z*oology, then the Scout office will steer you to that career group. If a group is not functioning in your area of interest, they will attempt to organize one. These groups usually meet twice a month with a volunteer specialist in the field working with the youth in a wide variety of ways. The philosophy is "Explore today for tomorrow." One such group in the Denver, Colorado, area, the Veterinarian Explorers, has been functioning for four years. This first-hand contact with professionals can help teens gain knowledge, make valid comparisons to their personal interests, and have a lot of fun.

Another school counselor was quick to say that the parent is the number one teacher of skills relating to the work experience such as writing out a check, preparing an income tax return, and seeing that the child has a social security number. Don't forget these important details.

DECIDING HOW TO REACH THE GOALS

When the child knows the answer to "What do I want to be?," the next question is "How do I reach my goal?" First, check out the requirements in the *Occupational Handbook* or with people in that field, then set about meeting them. School counselors can help again by guiding your child toward the best schools or training options in your city. Perhaps even the school system offers some training in that field. Gary decided his freshman year in high school to be a veterinarian. From that point on, his classes, part-time jobs, and most of his leisure reading focused on that goal. His experiences confirmed his choice, and by age twenty-five he was well-established in his career and doing post-doctoral work. Gary is an unusual case because few children know so early the perfect job fit, however, once the decision is made, efforts should be started to get maximum exposure, as Gary did, to the chosen field. Encourage your children to acquaint themselves with people in that occupation and search for part-time or volunteer work. Career changing is common in our society; few people stay in the same job until retirement. Show understanding if your children go through changes too.

Remember the caution of many career specialists: "A college education is no guarantee of occupational or financial success." Help your child think about all kinds of educational opportunities, from vocational and trade schools to armed services, junior colleges, and on the job training. Sadly, many college graduates experience unemployment and settle for work completely unrelated to their chosen profession. One enterprising young man took computer science at a technical center and did welding on the side, a skill he learned in high school. His welding business was successful enough to finance his continued schooling and completion of a computer science degree at a university. Encourage your children to think about two career choices—one that is practical and marketable and another career they really want to follow. This way the young adult may be worth twice as much on the job market.

Your child can investigate getting scholarship money and student loans. Such information can be obtained from high school counseling offices and colleges. Millions of dollars in scholarships and grants go unused every year because no one applies for the money. Not only do universities offer money, but also government, industry, fraternal, and other community groups award scholarships. Student loans from colleges are usually offered at lower interest rates and provide payment plans following graduation.

Above all, be a sounding board for questions, concerns, and anxieties. The confidence you have helped build in your child by nurturing independence and by teaching home management skills will carry over at this critical time too.

Index

Share your favorite incentives and work motivators with us; we welcome your comments and suggestions. If your ideas are used in a future book we will send you a free copy.

Sending your ideas gives permission for them to be published. Please be in touch with us c/o St. Martin's Press, 175 Fifth Avenue, New York, N.Y. 10010.

Bonnie McCullough
Sue Monson

To get other copies of this book, you can order them through your local bookstore, or directly from St. Martin's Press, c/o Publishers Book and Audio, P.O. Box 120159, Staten Island, New York 10312.

ORDER FORM

Please send _____ copies of 401 WAYS TO GET YOUR KIDS TO WORK AT HOME @ $8.95 plus postage and handling charges of $1.50 for the first book and $.75 for each additional book. (0-312-301472)

Please send _____ copies of BONNIE'S HOUSEHOLD BUDGET BOOK @ $7.95 plus postage and handling charges of $1.50 for the first book and $.75 for each additional book. (0-312-009925)

Please send _____ copies of BONNIE'S HOUSEHOLD ORGANIZER @ $5.95 plus postage and handling charges of $1.50 for the first book and $.75 for each additional book. (0-312-009925)

Please send _____ copies of TOTALLY ORGANIZED @ $11.95 plus postage and handling charges of $1.50 for the first book and $.75 for each additional book. (0-312-807473)

Please send _____ copies of 76 WAYS TO GET ORGANIZED FOR CHRISTMAS @ $3.95 plus postage and handling charges of $1.50 for the first book and $.75 for each additional book. (0-312-713266)

Name _____

Address _____

City _____ *State* _____ *Zip* _____

For group orders of 10 or more copies, please call 1-800-221-7945, ext. 530.

Printed in the United States
1441600001B/353